# AT THE BREAKING OF BREAD

## Homilies on the Eucharist

Edited by Patrick Jones

VERITAS

*First published 2005 by*
Veritas Publications
7/8 Lower Abbey Street
Dublin 1
Ireland
Email publications@veritas.ie
Website www.veritas.ie

ISBN 1 85390 910 6

Copyright © the individual contributors, 2005

10 9 8 7 6 5 4 3 2 1

The material in this publication is protected by copyright law. Except as may be permitted by law, no part of the material may be reproduced (including by storage in a retrieval system) or transmitted in any form or by any means, adapted, rented or lent without the written permission of the copyright owners. Applications for permissions should be addressed to the publisher.

A catalogue record for this book
is available from the British Library.

Printed in the Republic of Ireland
by Betaprint, Dublin

Veritas books are printed on paper made from the wood pulp of managed forests. For every tree felled, at least one tree is planted, thereby renewing natural resources.

# Contents

Introduction     7

## The Lord's Day

Concentrate on Keeping the Faith     13
*Pádraig Walsh*

A Rich Tradition     16
*Eoin Mangan*

Knowing Our Hunger     20
*Martin Hogan*

Go in Peace     24
*Niall Howard*

## Eucharist and the Human Condition

Solidarity     29
*Aidan Troy CP*

Eucharistic Love     33
*Tom Clancy*

Bread for the Hungry     35
*Frank Murray*

The Glory of God Veiled in the Eucharist     39
*Aidan Troy CP*

## THANKSGIVING

Saying Thanks     45
*Tony Flannery CSsR*

Why Should We Stay?     48
*Tom Clancy*

Thanksgiving     52
*Tony Flannery CSsR*

## REAL PRESENCE

Who Do You Say That I Am?     57
*Tom Clancy*

The Real Presence     60
*Silvester O'Flynn OFMCap*

Be Not Afraid     65
*Eamon Graham*

Christ-Mass     67
*Tom Clancy*

## WORD AND SACRIFICE

Servant of the Word     73
*John Watts*

On Understanding Sacrifice     76
*Eamon Graham*

Embracing Sacrifice     79
*Eamon Graham*

BREAD OF LIFE, CUP OF SALVATION

An Invitation to the Feast     85
*Tony Flannery CSsR*

They Collected the Scraps     88
*Frank Murray*

Pearl of Great Price     92
*Ken O'Riordan*

The Blood of the New Covenant     95
*Silvester O'Flynn OFMCap*

Communion, Our Peace     100
*Ken O'Riordan*

SERVICE

Eucharist – a Life of Service     105
*Dermot Lane*

Eucharist Leads to Service     109
*John Watts*

'Give Them Something To Eat Yourselves'     112
*Silvester O'Flynn OFMCap*

## Eucharist and Justice

| | |
|---|---|
| The Eucharist and Justice<br>*Dermot Lane* | 119 |
| Like Jesus Who Serves<br>*Martin Hogan* | 124 |
| Strength to Serve<br>*John Watts* | 128 |
| Blessed Are You Who Are Poor<br>*Dermot Lane* | 132 |

## Eucharist and Mission

| | |
|---|---|
| Receiving Eternal Life<br>*Aidan Troy CP* | 141 |
| From East to West<br>*Martin Hogan* | 146 |
| The Table of Inclusion<br>*Frank Murray* | 150 |
| Communion and Ecumenism<br>*Ken O'Riordan* | 154 |
| Mission<br>*Gerry French SSC* | 157 |

# Introduction

*At the Breaking of Bread...* Like the disciples we too have recognised Jesus the Lord at the table of Eucharist. That table has provided rich nourishment in word and sacrament. The word has been in human words even though the mystery is divine. The words have been liturgical, prayer texts, old and new. They have been biblical, proclaimed and explained. The explanation, a breaking open of the word, is homily, originally meaning an informal conversation but in liturgy, through the course of the liturgical year, a setting forth of the mysteries of faith and the standards of the Christian life on the basis of the sacred text (*General Introduction to the Lectionary*, 24).

The homily is "an exposition of some aspect of the readings from Sacred Scripture or of another text from the Ordinary or from the Proper of the Mass of the day and should take into account both the mystery being celebrated and the particular needs of the listeners" (*General Instruction of the Roman Missal*, 65). The homilies in this collection are inspired by the Scripture readings but in a special way by the sacred mysteries that are being celebrated. They are not just homilies *at* Eucharist but *on* Eucharist.

St Justin in his description of the Sunday gathering, written around the year 150, tells us that after the readings, the one who was presiding exhorted his hearers to live by the splendid things that they had heard. A beautiful description but also a reminder that the homily has limits. As well as homilies we also need other occasions for instruction and catechesis on the Eucharist.

Homilies are not written in the abstract. A brief account of the background to this collection is important.

The Year of the Eucharist, which began in October 2004, prompted this book of homilies. The letter of the late Pope John Paul II, *Mane nobiscum Domine* (*Remain with us, Lord*) suggested major themes and words about the Eucharist and this lead to a commissioning of homilies inspired by words like thanksgiving, sacrifice, meal, communion, solidarity and justice. But homilies are written and spoken on specific occasions and an indication of the Sunday or feast is included in the introduction to the homilies in this collection. Several are homilies for Holy Thursday and the solemnity of the Body and Blood of Christ (Corpus Christi), very obvious occasions for preaching on the Eucharist. But other Sundays present the opportunity for the homily to be on a Eucharistic theme. The gospel on the five Sundays, 17th to 21st in Ordinary Time, in the Year of Mark (Year B), is from the sixth chapter of St John's gospel, with its many references to Jesus as the Bread of Life. Most of the homilies we hear are at Mass and the Eucharist itself may be the subject of the homily on many Sundays and – it is important to add – on many weekdays.

Fourteen people have contributed thirty-five homilies. There is a variety of style, length and topic. Ancient words mingle with contemporary expressions. But there is a common Eucharistic faith expressed in the words that group the homilies, though words are inadequate to fully express this *mysterium fidei*.

Another person's homily is still the other person's. But we can hear them as a homily since we were not the hearers in the first place. And the thoughts and words of another person's homily or our own previous homilies are part of what we bring to the next homily.

A homily is spiritual nourishment. Read these homilies. Go back to the Scripture readings that may have prompted them. Because they are about the Eucharist, be familiar with the liturgical texts of the Mass.

Just as the homily at Mass moves us forward to the Liturgy of the Eucharist, may these homilies bring us to say: it is right to give God praise and thanks.

# The Lord's Day

Ninth Sunday in Ordinary Time: Year C

# Concentrate on Keeping Faith

*Pádraig Walsh CC, St John's, Tralee, Co Kerry*

*Taking part in the Mass, Sunday after Sunday, is essential nourishment on life's journey. The scripture references below are scattered throughout the year. Ezekiel 36:28 is heard at the Easter Vigil and on Thursday, 20th Week, Year II; (Matthew 6:9) Our Father is read on Tuesday, 1st Week of Lent and Thursday, 11th Week; Jesus in the synagogue at the Chrism Mass (Luke 4:16) on Holy Thursday and on 10 January; I am the vine (John 15:5) is read on 5th Sunday of Easter, Year B and on the Wednesday of that week as well as on several feasts of saints; The passage about the healthy and the sick (Matthew 9:12-13) is read on 10th Sunday in Ordinary Time, Year A and on Friday, 13th Week.*

As a priest, I frequently meet people at occasions like weddings or funerals and often they talk about religion or their own faith. Generally people are very open and honest. Some have reasons for going to Sunday Mass, while others have reasons for not attending!

One of the reasons people give for not attending is this: 'I pray better on my own!' Of course, nobody can argue with such a statement. On our own we have quietness and peace, with few distractions. We can reflect on life or the scriptures. We can pray for ourselves or the needs of others.

But Sunday Mass is different. Though we are all individuals, at Mass we gather as a Christian community. In the Old Testament, we read from the prophet Ezekiel, 'You shall be my people and I will be your God.' (Ezekiel 36: 28) In the New Testament Jesus taught us how to pray with the words 'Our Father' (Matthew 6:9), not 'My Father'. Though Jesus went off to pray by himself he also went to the synagogue on the Sabbath. So while our faith is personal, it also has a communal dimension. Therefore while we can pray well on our own, it is important that we also gather and pray as a community. That is what we do at our Sunday Mass.

Another reason people give is: 'Sure I can still be a good Catholic and not go to Mass!' We all know that living by the commandments, living by the values of Jesus and following his example is the way Catholics are supposed to live. He invited us to be radical in the way we live, to turn the other cheek, to forgive our enemies and to do good to those who hate us. Likewise he said to us, 'Do this in memory of me.' Catholic living and Catholic worship are meant to go hand in hand. Daily living and our celebration of the Mass need not be seen as a choice between doing one or the other. The Mass is a celebration of the love and mercy of God for each one of us. It puts before us the standard of Catholic living, which comes from Jesus. The Mass is not seen as an optional extra, but essential nourishment for our journey through life. The unity of life and the Eucharist is best symbolised as, 'I am the vine and you are the branches ... cut off from me you can do nothing!' (John 6:5)

Some people say they don't go to Mass because our churches are filled with hypocrites! Whatever about hypocrites, they are filled with sinners – many people with faults and failings, people who sin despite their best intentions. But wasn't that the ministry of Jesus? 'It is not the healthy who need the doctor but the sick... I did not come to call the virtuous but sinners'. (Matthew 9:12-13) This is best summed up in the phrase – 'The Church is not a hotel for the saints but a hospital for the sinners!'

Others say they don't go because they get nothing out of it. But is Mass one of those things that we are always supposed to get something from? We send a sympathy card to someone; what do we get out of that? We visit an elderly relative in a nursing home; what do we get out of that? We spend some time with our family on a Sunday; we don't always get something from that. Many of these things we do because we are part of a family, or a community. Sometimes what we do, is thoughtful, or kind or good for the other person. To ask what is in it for me might be the wrong question to ask.

The Sunday Mass is not something that is always perfect or that we are bursting to attend every weekend, yet our presence is important because we belong to a Christian community. Together we acknowledge our doubts, our anxieties, our sinfulness and our pain, but we also celebrate the love and mercy of God for each one of us, and the hope that only Christ can bring to our lives.

Ninth Sunday in Ordinary Time: Year B

# A Rich Tradition

*Canon Eoin Mangan PP, Cahirciveeen, Co. Kerry*

We have inherited a rich tradition. The Mass has had several names over the past two thousand years, each contributing to our understanding of this mystery. The Acts of the Apostles tell us that the first Christians met in their houses for 'the breaking of bread', the oldest name for the Eucharist. This reading, Acts 2:42-47 is read on 2nd Sunday of Easter, Year A.

What's in a name? The very mention of a certain name can arouse the deepest emotions in our hearts. We love to repeat the name of someone dear to us as a way of keeping their memory alive. Irish poets gave many names to the country they loved in order to inspire sentiments of patriotism and love. The Mass, too, has had many names down the centuries, and each name gives us a valuable insight into the meaning of the Mass.

The earliest name given to the Mass was 'The Breaking of Bread'. At the Last Supper Jesus took bread, broke it and gave it to his disciples. Sharing a meal with someone is a sign of friendship, welcome and solidarity. Breaking bread with his disciples was Jesus' way of uniting them with himself in the closest possible way. Later, the disciples at Emmaus recognised the Lord in the breaking of bread, and every time the early Christians gathered for the breaking of bread they were renewing their intimate connection with the Lord. An added meaning in this name for the Mass is the symbolism of the Body of Christ broken on the Cross for the sake of humankind. It is the Bread Broken for a New World, transforming our broken lives into the wholeness of the Risen Body of Christ. This name is closely linked with 'The Lord's Supper' and 'Sacred Meal'.

'Eucharist' is arguably the name used most to describe the Mass over the years. Eucharist is based on a Greek word, meaning to give thanks. The whole celebration is a thanksgiving sacrifice. We have so much to give thanks for: from the beginning of Mass when we receive forgiveness for our sins, through the Liturgy of the Word telling us of all the wonderful deeds of God on our behalf, to the gift of the Lord's presence and on to the final blessing giving us strength and grace for the coming week.

The Irish word for the Mass is '*Aifreann*' from the Latin word for offering. We offer the sacrifice of the Mass, which is the sacrifice of Christ on the Cross. As Christ offered himself to the Father we unite ourselves with that offering. Of course, to make this really fruitful in our lives we must sacrifice something of ourselves. We are not silent spectators at the Mass. We bring our whole lives, our troubles, our hopes, our fears, our successes, our failures, our joys and our sorrows, and we offer them sincerely along with the offering of Christ. *Aifreann*, then, holds a great depth of meaning.

The word Mass itself comes from the final words of the Mass in Latin: '*Ite Missa est.*' These words were the words of mission to the people sending them out in peace to love and serve the Lord. They summed up everything that had gone before, begging those who had celebrated the Mass to put into practice in their lives everything they had learned: God's love in sending His Son, the Death and Resurrection of Christ, his communion with us in the Real Presence, and the desire to imitate him in daily living.

The early Church kept the meaning of the Eucharist a secret from outsiders for fear of Roman persecution. When we proclaim the Mystery of Faith we make bold public proclamation of what we believe. We proclaim that the Eucharist is truly our 'Lord and God'. We proclaim the Death, Resurrection and Second Coming of Christ. We proclaim that Christ has destroyed death, restored life and will come again in glory. We proclaim that Christ is the Saviour of the World. In the Real Presence of Christ in the Eucharist the whole mystery of our Christian Faith is renewed and made active in our lives.

'*Agape*' is another Greek word meaning 'love'. At the Last Supper Jesus showed the depth of his love. In the first place he washed the disciples' feet as sign of his love for them and as an example to them. The Mass is not for ourselves alone: it is to be an incentive to us to 'Go in peace to love and serve the Lord', especially through loving and serving our neighbours and those in need. Eucharistic devotion, therefore, is both inward-looking (adoration of the real presence of the Lord) and outward-looking (putting into practice the example of love given to us by the Lord). The words 'Do this in memory of me' can be applied not only to the celebration of the Mass, but to every good and living deed done by the Lord.

# A Rich Tradition

Though the essential elements have remained the same, the structure of the Mass has changed and evolved during the centuries. Therefore, there are different rites of the Mass, for example, the Roman rite, the Greek rite, the Syrian rite. The Mass has been celebrated in different languages. At first it was celebrated in Aramaic, then in Greek and later in Latin. It is now celebrated in more than a thousand languages.

During the centuries the Mass has been celebrated in different places: in the homes of Christians, in the catacombs, in simple parish churches, in great cathedrals and basilicas, in concentration camps and in prison cells. It has been celebrated at times with great simplicity and at times with magnificent ceremony.

These differences as regards terms of description, places of celebration, language and rite do not affect the essence of the Mass or imply infidelity to the instruction of Jesus. Rather, they have enriched the Mass and underline the esteem in which Christians have held the Mass from the beginning. For they show that Christians have desired to implement Jesus' instruction in their own circumstances and in accordance with their own cultural traditions.

When we examine our own heritage of faith we find that the Mass has always been at the centre of the faith of the people. Many of our traditional prayers stress the importance of the Mass and the esteem in which it was held. This love for the Mass and fidelity to it were maintained even in penal times. Mass was celebrated in private houses or in secluded places in the country where shelters were erected and the 'Mass rock' served as an altar.

# Body and Blood of Christ (Corpus Christi): Year A

## Knowing Our Hunger

*Martin Hogan PC, Lecturer in Scripture,
Mater Dei Institute, Dublin*

*Having realised that we do not live on physical bread alone, we attend to deeper hungers and thirsts. In communion with Jesus in the Eucharist we are urged to a communion with his values. Though this reflection was prepared for the feast of the Body and Blood of Christ (Corpus Christi), Year A, the serious implications of communion are true for every Mass.*

The issue of obesity has been in the news in recent weeks. A lot of concern is being expressed in particular about children who are overweight. Measures are being looked at to encourage children to eat more healthily. There is a growing recognition that children need to be helped to choose well when it comes to what they eat and how often they eat. In past generations people ate because they were hungry. Nowadays there can be a tendency to eat for the sake of eating. This is one of the downsides of our age of relative plenty and prosperity. In the course of our history as a people we have known much leaner times, when obesity, especially in children, was the least of our problems.

## Knowing our Hunger

In today's first reading, Moses calls on the people to remember the time in the wilderness when they were hungry. They had left Egypt, a land of plenty thanks to the life-giving presence of the river Nile, and entered a wilderness where food was scarce. Moses reminded them that in those scarce and lean times, the Lord provided for them. Moses wants the people to remember that when their own resources had run out in the wilderness, it was the Lord who kept them going. What kept them alive during those lean years was not so much the physical food that was miraculously provided, but rather the Lord who provided that food. There was a lesson here that the people needed to remember when the time of plenty came round again, as it would when they entered the promised land. That lesson is summed up in the statement in today's first reading, 'We do not live on bread alone, but on every word that comes from the mouth of God'.

In times of plenty, it is easy to forget that we do not live on bread alone. When there are so many opportunities to satisfy our physical appetites, we can easily lose touch with the deeper appetites in our lives. In times when we have the resources to make great material progress, our spiritual progress can suffer. The Book of Deuteronomy presents Moses as being very aware of this danger and as wanting to warn the people about it. Jesus was very aware of it too. In commenting on the seed that is choked by thorns, he refers to how the lure of wealth and the desire for other things can come in and choke the word. However, neither Moses nor Jesus advocated going back to the wilderness in response to this danger. Neither of them led a movement into the desert as a way of dealing with the downside of plenty. Both of them, however, stressed that in the midst of plenty we need to remember that we do not live on physical bread alone. In such times we need to attend to the deeper hungers and thirsts in our lives.

In today's Gospel reading, Jesus presents himself as the one who can ultimately satisfy those deeper hungers and thirsts. He speaks of himself as the living bread come down from heaven. It is above all in the Eucharist that Jesus offers himself to us as food and drink for the satisfying of those deeper hungers and thirsts. In coming to the Eucharist we are opening our hearts to the one who declares that he is the Bread of Life and who invites us to take and eat. If someone were to ask us why we go to Mass, we would have to say that we go to Mass because Jesus as Bread of Life has called on us to take and eat. We go to Mass because, in the words of today's Gospel reading, Jesus has said to us, 'If you do not eat the flesh of the Son of Man and drink his blood, you will not have life in you'.

It was at the last supper that Jesus first called on his disciples to take and eat, to take and drink, having identified the bread as his body given for them and the wine as his blood poured out for them. At the last supper Jesus gave himself to his disciples as food and drink. At every Eucharist Jesus does the same for subsequent generations of disciples. The feast of Corpus Christi reminds us that the Lord's invitation to take and eat is as strong today as it was two thousand years ago. We come to Mass because we recognise Jesus as the Bread of Life who alone can respond to the deepest longings of our hearts, because, in the words of St Paul in today's second reading, we want to be in communion with the body and blood of Christ, our real food and real drink.

To be in communion with Jesus in the Eucharist is to be in communion with the values that he lived by and died for. When Jesus said to his disciples at the last supper, 'take and eat', he was at the same time calling on them to stand where he stood, to live the communion they shared at the table when they left the room and headed out to face Jesus' enemies. However, the communion the disciples shared with Jesus at table was almost immediately shattered as they abandoned him at the moment of his arrest. When we take the bread and the cup of the Eucharist we too are declaring that we want to imbibe all Jesus stood for. We are committing ourselves to live by his values, to walk in his way, to be shaped by his Spirit. We come to Mass not only to receive from Jesus, but also to give to him. In that sense, coming to Mass is a serious business. It is making a statement that we will stand with the Lord in all our comings and goings.

## Ninth Sunday in Ordinary Time: Year A

# Go in Peace

*Niall Howard, Chaplain, Coláiste Na Sceilge, Cahirciveen, Co Kerry.*

*We must imitate the mysteries we celebrate. Through listening to God, through attention to the words and actions of the Mass we are called to live our Christian calling.*

A joke without a punchline is no good, and hearing five Lotto numbers called out and then missing the last one is far from satisfactory! We are people who gather together to worship at Eucharist, to hear God's Word and receive Christ's Body and Blood. But it doesn't end when we leave the Church. Just as the sixth Lotto number is crucial for deciding whether we are millionaires or not, likewise the dismissal at the end of Mass is crucial to our time of prayer and to our lives as Christians. The most powerful dismissal is 'Go in peace to love and serve the Lord'. Being a good Catholic isn't just about the Sunday morning hour, because we are not just spectators – we are called to action at each Mass.

But how do we go in peace to love and serve the Lord? Maybe we could imitate the mysteries we celebrate and imitate the various aspects of the Mass.

As we are welcomed at the beginning of the celebration of the Eucharist, so too we are called to welcome others – friend and stranger, Irish and asylum-seeker, settled and Traveller. Jesus accepts us, and we are called to do the same.

We ask for God's forgiveness when we pray the Confiteor and the 'Lord have mercy', and we are ourselves called to go in peace to ask forgiveness of others and forgive those who have hurt or belittled us.

We hear the word of God, but sometimes we are so distracted that we really listen to only a line or two. Why not go in peace and take a Mass leaflet and read over the readings again, so as to continue to deepen your own faith.

We always take the chance to pray for our needs and the needs of others in the Prayer of the Faithful. But if we pray for the Church on Sunday, why not see how we can use our talents over the week by being more involved in our own parish? We pray for the sick and the housebound, so why not go in peace to visit them and pray with them and bring them Holy Communion?

We pray for justice in the world, but we are called to be just and honest in our own dealings with others and in our care for creation.

At the offertory, we present gifts of bread and wine. The Gospel reminds us that when we come to the altar and remember that we are not at peace with our brother or sister, we should first go and be reconciled with our brother and sister and then come to worship God. Is there someone with whom I need to mend fences?

In the Rite of Ordination, when the priest accepts the chalice and paten for the first time he is told to 'Know what you are doing, and imitate the mystery you celebrate: model your life on the mystery of the Lord's cross'. Do we always take the time to know what we are doing? Is our life modelled on the Lord's cross or do we settle for a comfortable, settled life?

During the Eucharist Prayer, we kneel as the Body of Christ and then the Blood of Christ are elevated in silence. So during the week maybe we could try a bit more to make time for our own personal prayer. The Church is always open during the day, so why not drop in for a while for prayer and adoration before Christ in the Blessed Sacrament?

At each Mass we pray for peace and share with others the peace of Christ. But we are also commissioned to go in peace and do all we can to bring that peace of Christ to our homes, our workplaces and our community.

At Communion time, the Body of Christ is shared with us and we come forward to accept it. In what we do during the rest of the week we are called to live our lives in a manner fitting for such a gift.

But we are also, as believers, called to be more rooted in our community for faith, in our Church - the Body of Christ. Hence, as St Augustine said, we are called to become what we receive.

Mass isn't just a weekend thing, and it isn't just a weekly faith injection. For us, the Mass is the summit of the past week's living, and the source for the coming week's living.

We are all asked to live our Christian calling to the full so at the end of this celebration of the Eucharist, may we go in peace, to love and serve the Lord.

# EUCHARIST
# AND THE HUMAN
# CONDITION

## Tenth Sunday in Ordinary Time: Year A

# Solidarity

*Aidan Troy CP, Holy Cross, Ardoyne, Belfast.*

*The Eucharist is a celebration of an intimate bond between God and humankind. It is also a celebration of the bond that exists among humankind. The prophet Hosea proclaimed, 'What I want is love, not sacrifice.' This is a call to reach out, to include; Jesus sitting at table with the tax collectors and sinners is a good example of such solidarity. The readings, Hosea 6:3-6 with Psalm 49 and Matthew 9:9-13 are read on 10th Sunday in Ordinary Time, Year A.*

I am a sinner. This is not a boast. I am not proud of it. But it is an essential part of who I am. Because I am broken in this fundamental way I dare not look down on others who are injured, broken or even just different. Being a sinner makes me dependent, humble and sometimes afraid. Of the six billion of us inhabiting the planet the one character trait that we all have in common is our brokenness. The only One who has walked the earth free from this affliction is Jesus. But He took on our affliction, our brokenness.

Some months ago I was photographed at a political party dinner. The invitation was simple – please come and eat with us. Then an elected politician of a different political party wrote that he was profoundly dismayed and indeed very surprised to see that photograph in a local newspaper and that some parishioners raised the issue with him in equal dismay. Such comments represent the view of some good people. Those who are 'in' are respectable and careful. Those who are 'out' are better left there. But Jesus worked from a different model and had a dream for the poor, the sick, the excluded, the children and the broken – 'what I want is love, not sacrifice; knowledge of God, not holocausts.' (Hosea 6:6)

'Break' open the Mystery of the Eucharist and there is a Jesus who chose as one of his disciples a tax collector, a despised occupation, and a collaborator whose aim was to fill the coffers of the occupying Romans. To add insult to injury, Jesus went on not only to have contact with tax collectors and sinners, but went so far as to eat at their table. Would Jesus not have done better to have been more careful in both his choice of followers and the company he kept? There were so many respectable people around to chose from and to associate with. One day Jesus would pay with his life the supreme price of loving so widely, so much and so intensely.

'We are constantly tempted to reduce the Eucharist to our own dimensions, while in reality it is we who must open ourselves up to the dimensions of the Mystery.' (*Mane nobiscum Domine* (Remain with us, Lord), Apostolic Letter of Pope John Paul II, October 2004 N. 14). How true. But there is a price to be paid by us as there was by Jesus. It is so much safer to tailor the Eucharist to our own proportions. Mass is safe unless one listens to the challenge of the Eucharist, 'It is the impulse

## SOLIDARITY

which the Eucharist gives to the community for a practical commitment to building a more just and fraternal society.' (ibid. N.28) This will involve suffering to a greater or lesser degree.

'Naked suffering' (a term used by St Paul of the Cross, Founder of the Passionists) comes when even God seems to have deserted you. 'My God, my God, why have you abandoned me?' (Matthew 27:46). In our world even the name of God has lost its force. People we know to be good die the most painful of deaths. A parent loses a child to cot-death, for instance. Young men and women lose all hope and die by suicide. On the day our world celebrates love, St Valentine's Day, as I was coming down the scaffolding from Holy Cross Church tower a man asked what clothes the young boy hanging at the top was wearing. When I told him, 'That is my son' was his bald statement. In his eyes I saw abandonment, desolation and the question put to God, 'Why have you abandoned me?' When an hour later he cradled his dead seventeen-year-old son in his arms in the back of an ambulance we had Calvary again. This time it was George and Barney in place of Mary and Jesus. The suffering of death is intense and makes Resurrection seem distant.

Eucharist is giving until only blood and water remain. It is the broken host that carries the broken but healing Jesus. It takes a Crucified Jesus to love deeply 'crucified' people. Suffering people are His special choice. He does not ask whether you love Him. He begins by loving the person who is carrying the cross. There is only one Cross revealing a hidden link between suffering and Love. He feels at home with those who suffer and will never walk away from the broken-hearted. He wants to feed them with Himself. He described himself as a doctor sent to the sick.

Matthew's Gospel leads us to see that The Eucharist is not merely an expression of communion in the Church's life, but it is also a project of solidarity for all of humanity. In the celebration of the Eucharist the Church constantly renews her awareness of being a 'sign and an instrument' not only of intimate union with God but also of the unity of the whole human race. (*Mane nobiscum Domine,* 27) There is no private Mass; Eucharist always has a universal character and promotes communion, peace and solidarity in every situation. Our entry into the Mystery of the Eucharist is to humbly:

> Pay your sacrifice of thanksgiving to God
> and render him your votive offerings.
> Call on me in the day of distress.
> I will free you and you shall honour me.
> *(Psalm 49:14-15)*

Twenty-First Sunday in Ordinary Time: Year C

# Eucharistic Love

*Tom Clancy PP, Parish of the Holy Spirit, Dennehy's Cross, Cork*

> *In God's way of doing things, the Eucharist is ever creative, ever transformative. The Eucharist is a gift that shows God's generosity but it is impoverished if our response is not of service and love of our brothers and sisters. This homily was written for 21st Sunday in Ordinary Time, Year C, when the readings prompt us to think of the feast that Christ prepares is for everyone. In reaching out in love and service, people will come from east and west, north and south to the feast in the kingdom of God (Luke 13: 22-30). Such a message is suitable for many Sundays and weekdays.*

It seems to be a lesson that God never learned. Human experience teaches us that people never appreciate what they get for nothing. The accepted wisdom is that there should be at least a nominal charge for goods or for the use of facilities.

Yet God works from a different agenda. He freely and unconditionally gives the most extraordinary gift of his son to an ungrateful human race who crucify him. More extraordinarily still, he continues to give this Son in the Eucharist to a people who are often indifferent or casual to the wonder of his generosity. Communion is an opportunity to enter into a profound relationship with Jesus, a mutual abiding that helps to satisfy our deepest human yearnings. Yet, we can be so casual. Why is God so generous to the undeserving?

Because the motive of God's gift giving is not our worthiness but our need. It is not that we have a right to Eucharist but we have a need of it, a need that cannot be fulfilled in any other way.

In God's way of doing things, the Eucharist is ever creative, ever transformative. It can gradually change us from anxious, self-centred, dormant members of the believing community into disciples, enthused witnesses to the Risen Lord, ever present in our lives.

Such is the power of Eucharistic love, God's love for us in the Eucharist and our willingness to be renewed. God's gift must not return to him empty. Of those to whom so much is given, a great deal is expected. The temptation is to frustrate the power of the Eucharist, to settle for a passive peripheral friendship with the Lord, to base our claim for salvation on having merely shared the Lord's table. 'We ate and drank in your company.'

This is not what the Eucharist is about. It demands that we go out to live in a communion of love, to love and serve the Lord in our brothers and sisters, to release into our world the healing love of the Lord. If such enduring, loving service does not flow from the Eucharist, God's gift of himself is impoverished. It is a frightening thought to frustrate the personal gift of the living God. Our destiny is to participate in its fulfilment.

# Eighteenth Sunday in Ordinary Time: Year C

## Bread for the Hungry

*Frank Murray, PP, Ferbane, Co. Offaly*

*Jesus, the Bread of Life, is the food for the many hungers of our human condition. Appreciating these experiences of hunger also helps us to understand the Eucharist as the Bread of Life. Having begun reading from the sixth chapter of St John about the feeding of the five thousand on the previous Sunday, 18th Sunday in Ordinary Time, Year B gives us a second extract on the Bread of Life.*

Sir, give us that Bread always
I am the Bread of Life
The one who comes to me will never be hungry.

The human heart contains great yearning. 'God has placed in human hearts a 'hunger' for his word' (*Mane nobiscum Domine*, 19).

The human heart has many hungers. The first hunger is for food, for our daily bread which lies at the heart of our world. So much of the world today sits with Lazarus at the gate of

## At the Breaking of Bread

Dives waiting for the scraps to fall from the table mountain of excess. As another diet book is published, my brother and sister sit famished in a world of plenty. Give us this day our daily bread, the Bread of Life to share with open hands and to feed the hungry heart of our world.

We hunger for the Bread of Life.

> 'The one who comes to me will never be hungry.'
> 'Sir, give us that Bread always.'

There is a great hunger in the human heart for freedom. We pine to dance to the music that will set us free. We want to be free from all tyranny of war and greed, the clenched fist, the wicked word, and the random violence of the darkness of the night. We long to be freed from fear, the fear of my own beauty and goodness and the fear of my own darkness and pain. We long for Jubilee time to break the fetters and loosen the chains of bondage. So many of our appetites enslave us to excess. We long for the appetite of freedom... free at last.

We hunger for the Bread of Life.

> 'The one who comes to me will never be hungry.'
> 'Sir, give us that Bread always.'

There is a deep hunger in the human heart for forgiveness. It is the call of our fractured and fragile selves for forgiveness. We wound ourselves, as we wound other people, often in our attempt to love them. We litter the landscape, pollute the skies, and poison the rivers and wells that give us life. Compulsive in our needs and greeds, unaware of the plank in our own eye, too often ready to throw the first stone, we are blind to the hurt we cause to others. The human heart pines for the rain of forgiveness like a dry weary land without water.

We hunger for the Bread of Life.

> 'The one who comes to me will never be hungry.'
> 'Sir, give us that Bread always.'

The human heart has a hunger for fidelity in the world of the broken promise; we long for a word that is our bond. We crave loyalty, commitment and people who won't let us down. Our hearts are torn by every broken home, every broken relationship and every broken dream. We fear the fickleness of forever. We want to believe in the possibility of permanence. We want to believe in the promise, made and lived for better or worse, for richer or poorer, in sickness and in health all the days of our life. The human heart hungers for the bread of fidelity.

We hunger for the Bread of Life.

> 'The one who comes to me will never be hungry.'
> 'Sir, give us that Bread always.'

There is a hunger in the human heart for friendship. It is the call of the heart for community, for communication, for a holy communion. We are not islands, isolated and insulated from each other. We are created needing completion in community and in family and therefore we are orientated for relationship. We belong and so there is a longing in the heart for affection and affirmation. We need others to know, accept, love and forgive the person we really are. We tire of wearing the mask of the public place, hiding our darkest fears and deepest hopes. We need to feed our famished hearts with friendship.

We hunger for the Bread of Life.

> 'The one who comes to me will never be hungry.'
> 'Sir, give us that Bread always.'

There is hunger in the human heart for fun, for gaiety and joy. Sin always wears the cross face of the frown. There is no joy or laughter in the heart of greed and bitterness, envy and lust. The terrorist never smiles. The face of war is the face of innocence, tear-stained and blood-stained. We long for the joy of grace and gratitude, simplicity and service and the child-like gift of laughter.

We hunger for the Bread of Life.

> 'The one who comes to me will never be hungry.'
> 'Sir, give us that Bread always.'

There is a hunger in the human heart for faith. In a godless world of the compulsive ego, speed and noise rob us of depth and serenity. We long for a God who gives our world a perspective of compassion. In the coarseness of the tabloid headline, our souls pine for a depth of gentle truth. We hunger for wordless prayer. In the randomness of a casual evil, we want to believe in the graciousness of Life. We long to have faith in a providential Carer who calls us to freedom and life and to the service of others. We need to have Faith in the Hope that is the gift of Love.

We hunger for the Bread of Life.

> 'The one who comes to me will never be hungry.'
> 'Sir, give us that Bread always.'

### Tenth Sunday in Ordinary Time: Year C

# The Glory of God Veiled in the Eucharist

*Aidan Troy CP, Holy Cross, Ardoyne, Belfast.*

*The story of the raising of the widow's son at Nain is one of the very familiar Gospel stories. When we hear it at a funeral, it reminds us that beyond the veil of death there is life. In the Eucharist the glory of Christ remains veiled but through this mystery, our faith leads into the depths of divine life. The story of the widow's son (Luke 7:11-17) is the Gospel of 10th Sunday in Ordinary Time, Year C. It is also read on Tuesday, 24th Week and sometimes at funerals.*

Michael was twenty months old. He was the youngest of four children. He was loved by parents, siblings and all who met him. He was one of those happy and outgoing children who was known and loved by all in the street.

He was blessed with good health. Then just after Christmas Michael's mother lifted him up one morning and he was dead. The ambulance, police, doctor, forensics all acted kindly and professionally. As a priest you see the question in people's eyes before it come to their lips, 'Why? It's not fair'. I had no ready answers and fewer explanations. I could just offer my time, bless the children and parents, say a prayer and be there. The postmortem was inconclusive, but the return of Michael's body for the wake was a huge comfort to all.

There would be no miracle in which I would touch the small white coffin and say, 'Young man, I tell you to get up'. It would have been pointless to have said to the parents, grandparents and relatives, old and young, 'Do not cry'. It doesn't work like that in the world we live in today. The parents and relatives begin to ask about the funeral and what should be done. Then you see something of the wonder of family support. The school choir from the siblings' school will come to sing at the Mass. Someone else wants to read, another wants to offer a prayer. A teddy bear is produced for the offertory procession. And all the while the lingering question, 'Why?' hangs there unanswered.

Luke helps us. He has a special interest in the resurrection of the dead. He alone among the Evangelists tells the story of the raising of the widow's son of Nain and his being given back to his mother. By this Luke portrays Jesus as a great prophet. He is in the line of Elijah and Elisha, both of whom restored life to the sons of widows. Elijah prays, 'Lord my God, may the soul of this child, I beg you, come into him again.' (1 Book of Kings 17:21) Against all the odds the mother receives back her child alive. The joy and relief can only be imagined and measured against the sorrow and suffering of the dead child as his funeral is prepared.

Luke sees Jesus as the Messiah fulfilling the prophecies of old. He tells those sent by John the Baptist enquiring about his Messianic role, 'the dead are raised to life.' (Luke 7:22) Luke gives us Jesus as another Elijah. Luke wants us to appreciate that Jesus is also a towering prophetic figure. Elijah lived during the reign of Aheb, King of Israel, almost nine hundred years before the coming of Jesus. As we know Elijah was believed to have entered heaven in a horse and chariot. He was expected to return.

Maybe I am cowardly, but I didn't use the texts of the widow's son of Nain or the wonders wrought by Elijah at Michael's funeral. To look into the eyes of parents and their children as they clasp the little white coffin makes all words difficult, even the Word of God.

In the face of death the first gift we have to offer is silent presence. To try to explain or to take away the pain and the tears, besides being impossible, is insensitive. The way a parent explains to a child what has happened when a loved one dies is full of rich theology. They tell it so simply. The dead one is with God, at peace, a star, a flower in God's Garden, an angel in God's choir, a helper in God's House. A little girl stopped me going into the house during the days of the wake to say she thought God was very unfair to have taken baby Michael. I asked her in what way. God didn't give Michael much time to play with his Christmas toys was her reply. Brilliant. Only a child could say this so innocently.

Of all the times when faith and the afterlife stands us in good stead it is in the face of the suffering of death. Be that the death of a baby or someone old, there is only one certainty; the person is safe. They are with God and as they closed their eyes in death the first sight that greeted them was the face of God. I believe this as deeply as I believe anything. Especially when the loved one has ended their own life in suicide it is so important to deal with the afterlife in terms of a welcoming

God. So many people would want to prolong the suffering of the bereaved by qualifying God's mercy and compassion. The thief crucified with Jesus must have hung onto the words, 'Indeed, I promise you, today you will be with me in paradise.' (Luke 23:43)

Even if I had the power given by God to restore the dead child to his parents a greater gift is knowing that even now the dead are raised. This is the true gift of God. This is the miracle. Eternal life is held out by our God who wants all to be saved. The care of Jesus is never absent even in events like world disasters or the death of a baby. The heart of Jesus goes out not just to the widow of Nain, but to mothers and fathers, brothers and sisters and to all. So often Jesus seems to be absent when needed most. But absent He is not. He asks us to reveal His presence by our presence, affection, silence, words, faith, hope and most of all, love. When the broken-hearted feel they can take no more, when numbness predominates, it is the responsibility of the believing community to carry them. When in my life I could not believe, I know others who cared about me and carried me in their hearts. They prayed the prayers I couldn't utter.

'In the Eucharist the glory of Christ remains veiled. The Eucharist is pre-eminently a *mysterium fidei*. Through the mystery of his complete hiddenness, Christ becomes a mystery of light, thanks to which believers are led into the depths of the divine life.' (John Paul II, *Mane nobiscum Domine*, N.11) It is only when we have stayed with the hidden Lord that Jesus as Light of our World emerges.

# THANKSGIVING

TWENTY-EIGHTH SUNDAY IN ORDINARY TIME: YEAR C

# SAYING THANKS

*Tony Flannery CSsR, Esker, Athenry, Co. Galway*

*The Eucharist – the word means thanksgiving – is our great prayer of thanksgiving. Saying thanks is very important. The story of the ten lepers is a powerful reminder of its importance. This Gospel story (Luke 17:11-19), with the story of Naaman, another victim of leprosy and one grateful for his healing (2 Kings 5:14-17) are read on 28th Sunday in Ordinary Time, Year C. We also hear this same Gospel on Wednesday, 32nd Week.*

The ten lepers were in a sad and sorrowful condition. It was a dreadful disease in those days, with little or no possibility of a cure. Since it was thought to be highly contagious people were terrified of lepers. They were outcasts. They had to avoid contact with people, except others who were infected like themselves. They even rang a bell to warn people that they were coming so that everyone could keep well away. As we can see from the first reading, it was a disease that affected all classes of society. Namaan was a high court official. But inevitably, like serious diseases in all ages, the poor were more vulnerable.

We know nothing about the ten lepers Jesus met, except they all had the disease and one of them was a Samaritan. Jews did not mix with Samaritans, but obviously among the diseased that prejudice had broken down. When you are battling for the short time of life that you have left, there is no time or energy for racial hatred.

Why did the nine not come back to give thanks to Jesus? There could have been many reasons. The condition of leprosy was so horrible, with an utter sense of hopelessness about the future, that when they found themselves cured they immediately wanted to forget about that part of their lives. Treat it as if it had been a bad dream that they had just woken from. And maybe it was a dream; maybe it had never really happened.

As lepers they hadn't been able to contact their families and friends. They must have felt an enormous urgency to run and tell them the good news, 'I was dead, and now I am alive'. When they got the disease their lives had come to a halt. Now that they were cured they had so much living to do, so much time to make up, so many things to achieve. All the old ambitions and desires of their earlier life had come flooding back. Rather than go back to Jesus and the reality of their sickness, they wanted to move on, to get on living again.

As a colony of lepers they had cared for each other, minded each other, were even oblivious to the differences of class and race. Sickness can often bring out the best in a person; make a person more aware and thoughtful of others. But when they got well all their old selfishness and self-centredness came flooding back.

## Saying Thanks

Jesus was hurt that only one returned to offer thanks. Saying thanks is important. It is one of these simple human gestures that spreads goodness and decency, that encourages and promotes the kind of attitudes that help make life more tolerable for all of us.

If we learn to say thanks the Eucharist will begin to take on a new meaning. It is the great prayer of thanksgiving. In our preparation for the Eucharist we need to come with hearts attuned to the goodness and beauty of the world, and with a fundamental sense of thankfulness for everything. Then the Mass will be a great prayer of thanksgiving for ourselves and for life.

## Twenty-first Sunday in Ordinary Time: Year B

# Why Should We Stay?

*Tom Clancy PP, Parish of the Holy Spirit, Dennehy's Cross, Cork*

*What Jesus said as recorded in the sixth chapter of St John was unacceptable to many. Why should we stay? Because the Eucharist is where we hear the Word and experience the miracle of feeding on the Bread of Life. The fifth and final extract from the series of Gospel readings from John 6 is read on 21st Sunday in Ordinary Time, Year B.*

The crowds were fed. Many had experienced the miracle. They had heard the Word Himself. They had heard Jesus teach with passion and conviction. All to no avail. The crowds slipped away rapidly. Everybody was gone; well almost everybody. It was certainly a depressing moment. Jesus eyeballed those who lingered.

'What about you, do you want to go away too?'

The tension was palpable. Peter replied:

'Lord, who shall we go to? You have the message of eternal life and we believe; we know that you are the Holy One of God.

Peter's answer seems to be too good to be true. Such a comprehensive reply was hardly formulated so succinctly on the

## Why Should We Stay?

spot. At the time, Peter undoubtedly voiced his own loyalty and incipient faith, as well as that of the other disciples. But his proclamation of Christ's divinity, 'You are the Holy One of God' may have been attributed later to Peter by the early Christian community, reflecting on what his profession of loyalty implied.

If Jesus were to pose the same question to the increasing numbers of today's struggling believers, to us gathered here for Eucharist and to those who come occasionally to the Table of the Lord, the answer might, in the Kerry tradition, take the form of another question, 'Why should we stay?'

We stay because the Eucharist is where we hear the Word and experience the miracle. The Word we hear is the message of eternal life:

> Yes, it is my Father's will that whoever sees the Son and believes in him shall have eternal life and that I shall raise him up on the last day.
> (John 6:40)

The miracle we experience is to receive the Bread of Life:

> For my flesh is real food and my blood is real drink.
> He who eats my flesh and drinks my blood lives in me
> and I live in him.
> (John 6:55-56)

This Eucharist is where we belong, where we are formed into God's people, where we are challenged to make a leap of faith and see ourselves as home hosts to the Risen Jesus truly present to us and within us.

## At the Breaking of Bread

Those who were fed by the multiplication of the loaves were very aware that they were God's people, bound together by their journey from Egypt, from slavery to freedom under the leadership of Moses. They were proud of their roots and content to live off them. But now they glimpsed that they stood on the threshold of a great leap forward. Jesus was proclaiming himself as the new Moses, not just a messenger leader from God, but the Son of God himself sent to teach and to lead and, above all that, to give himself as the true bread from heaven. What was on offer was an intimate, all absorbing share in the life of God himself, the fullness of eternal life.

It was an awesome prospect. For the majority, it was a step too far. They were content to remain God's chosen people, to continue to follow the Law and the Prophets that had served them in good stead. They knew where they stood. There was security in the certainty. Abraham, Isaac, Jacob and Moses were their guarantors of God's care. Why risk the great leap forward to this new relationship with God who was offering to entrust himself so totally to them?

They saw the treasure, but glimpsed the cost. They chose to stay as they were and not to risk accepting the invitation to share in this explosive miracle. They left him in droves.

What about us in our time? Do we want to go away?

Some glimpse the reality but, seeing a conflict with their lifestyles, choose the other way. Others may never have been given the gift of faith or perhaps it has died for them. God will come to them in another way in his loving care. What of us gathered here in faith, hope and love searching for the God who is forever seeking us? Sometimes, perhaps, we receive the treasure without realising its creative power, its transforming spirit. We fail to realise that the Risen Jesus who comes to us

## Why Should We Stay?

in the Eucharist is the one sent to bring good news to the poor, to proclaim liberty to captives. To receive him is to be singed by the fire of his Spirit. Eucharist is not just about being fed with the true Bread from heaven. It is about all the family, feeding the hungry, healing the hurt, consoling the bereaved, building cells of justice and peace. This is what Eucharist enables us to do. The Eucharist is the transmission system of the enabling power of God's love. To receive it is to risk being changed every time.

Will we risk it or will we go away? Hopefully, we will stay where we belong as hearers of his Word and members of his Eucharistic family.

## Twenty-Eighth Sunday in Ordinary Time: Year B

# Thanksgiving

*Tony Flannery CSsR, Esker, Athenry, Co. Galway*

*Our response to the gift of generosity and love of Jesus given to us in the Eucharist must be thanksgiving. The rich man (Mark 10:17-30) was too attached to his possessions. The more we have, the more we tend to take things for granted and the less thankful we can be. This Gospel story we read on 28th Sunday in Ordinary Time, Year B.*

We spend a great deal of our lives trying to avoid a confrontation with ourselves. Modern life provides us with plenty of opportunity to do so. I was doing visitation in preparation for a parish mission. The particular house I was approaching looked opulent. I was surprised to discover that it was home to a young couple, with three small children. They were both successful business people. Since they were at their evening meal I tried to excuse myself, state my business quickly, and go. But they were warm and friendly, and insisted that I join them. The husband had returned the previous evening from a trip to the Far East, where in between business meetings he had managed a few days with an old school pal who was a missionary in the Philippine Islands. He told us how he had been shocked by the poverty of the people there. Then he became quiet for a moment, and, turning to me, said: 'I didn't feel good last night coming back to all this [he gestured around at his lovely house]; we have so much and they have so little.'

I didn't comment. What he had said was true, and I didn't want to demean his statement with platitudes. I could see that his wife was uncomfortable with the twist the conversation had taken. She was much too polite to tell him to keep quiet. Instead she got up and began to collect the plates. In doing so she managed to interrupt the flow of conversation. Then, before she turned to go to the kitchen she said to her husband; 'Darling, you can't afford to think about these things; that's just the way things are.' She did not want to be confronted with herself and her lifestyle. None of us do. But that is what Jesus did with the rich young man. And the story tells us that the young man backed away from the confrontation. He is the only example in the Gospels of someone who failed to respond when Jesus issued his call to follow him.

In the Gospel, understanding of life to be wealthy is a dangerous state. When we are well-off we can easily come to love our riches. Jesus could recognise that the young man has become possessed by his wealth, and he wanted to set him free from his addiction to possessions. The strange anomaly about the human personality is that the more we have the more we take everything for granted, and the less thankful we are. When we have enough, but are not burdened with excess, we are more likely to have a sense of gratitude.

## At the Breaking of Bread

In the Eucharist, when we experience the generosity and the love of Jesus, we are confronted once again with ourselves. We are challenged to let go of our clinging to material possessions and to focus instead on the deeper realities of life. If we can do that we will be better able to enter into the sense of gratitude that is at the heart of the Eucharist.

# REAL PRESENCE

## Twenty-First Sunday in Ordinary Time: Year A

# Who Do You Say That I Am?

*Tom Clancy PP, Parish of the Holy Spirit, Dennehy's Cross, Cork*

*The question to Peter is one we should answer in the context of Mass. Who is the Jesus of Eucharist? As Peter answered, we can say that in Eucharist we meet Jesus, the Christ, the Son of the living God. This also helps us to know our own identity as well. The Gospel, Matthew 16:13-20, is read on 21st Sunday in Ordinary Time, Year A and is used on feasts of St Peter and saints who were his successor as Bishop of Rome. A longer version is read on Thursday, 18th Week.*

Who do you say I am?

Every now and again at a funeral or a wedding, in a hospital or a school, perhaps, somebody says to me in a friendly but curious way, 'And who are you now, Father?' Is it my name, they want? Maybe.

Maybe I want to know the link. Why am I there? Am I related? Am I a friend? Occasionally, somebody intervenes and says, 'He is our parish priest.' Others say, 'He is one of the

Clancys that had the pubs'. Others may say kindly, 'He taught my son mathematics.' And so on.

How would you describe me?

It doesn't matter really.

How would you describe yourself?

By your parents or your children or your spouse.

By what you have achieved.

By what you own.

By your friends, your politics or your sporting involvements.

It would depend a bit on the context.

When Jesus asked Peter, 'Who do you say I am?' his reply could have been:

A carpenter from Nazareth.

A wandering preacher.

A miracle worker.

Mary's one and only.

A cousin of the Baptist preacher.

Jesus was looking for something more. Who was He really? Did Peter realise? His true identity was the Son of God. That was the essential and Peter knew it. But how could Peter be so sure? God has given him the gift of faith and Peter had spent enough time with jesus to be sure of that faith and able to articulate it.

When Jesus was reassured that Peter was on the right track, he entrusted to his care the treasure which is the Church.

The Church was to live and keep alive that faith in Jesus as Son of God, to nurture it, to hand it on from generation to generation, and in Peter's case, even to die for it.

## Who Do You Say That I Am?

The source and the summit of the life and mission of that church is the Eucharist. It is where we can spend time with Jesus like Peter did, getting to know who he really is, growing in friendship daily. This is where Jesus really is. We speak of the 'real' presence not in an exclusive way, as if we were suggesting that the other ways in which Jesus is present were not real.

We emphasise this presence par excellence where Jesus becomes substantially present, whole and entire, in the reality of his body and blood. Faith asks us to come to the Eucharist fully aware that we are approaching Christ himself. When we spend time with Jesus as Peter did, our faith can blossom like his. We become convinced that Jesus is Son of God, that one of our friends is Son of God. Then, when we ask ourselves who we are and why we are here, we know and we can describe ourselves: 'I am a friend and follower of Jesus of Nazareth, Son of God.'

This is our reassuring identity. It is the other side of the coin of knowing who Jesus is.

'Who do you say that I am?'

# Body and Blood of Christ (Corpus Christi): Year A

# The Real Presence

*Silvester O'Flynn OFMCap, Holy Trinity, Mathew Quay, Cork*

*Jesus tells us in chapter 6 of St John's Gospel that he is the living bread come down from heaven; the bread is his flesh for the life of the world. St Paul writes of the bread as a communion with the body of Christ, the blessing cup as a communion with the blood of Christ. We profess this when we speak of the real presence. John 6:51-58 is the Gospel for the feast of the Body and Blood of Christ (Corpus Christi), Year A. It is also read on 20th Sunday in Ordinary Time, Year B. The Pauline reference is the response to the psalm on Holy Thursday. 1 Cor 10:16-17 is read on Corpus Christi, Year A.*

The Feast of the Body and Blood of Christ is a celebration of the presence of Jesus Christ in the Blessed Eucharist. It is an astounding belief. We would not dare to hold this belief except that it is based on the very words of Jesus himself.

> I am the living bread which has come down from heaven.

# The Real Presence

> Anyone who eats this bread will live for ever;
> and the bread that I shall give
> in my flesh, for the life of the world.

Our belief in the presence of Jesus in the Blessed Eucharist is based on the words of Jesus, accepted in faith.

Scientific analysis would give us no grounds for faith. A chemical analysis of the bread or wine taken before the consecration would yield the same results as analysis taken after the consecration. What we call the accidents of bread and wine remain the same. The colour, shape, texture, taste and chemical components remain unchanged. Our belief is that the substance has been changed into the presence of Jesus Christ. We call it transubstantiation, change of substance.

If Jesus' body had been subjected to scientific testing while he was on earth, the results would have shown a human body. There would have been no material indication of the divine presence. That is how it is with the Blessed Eucharist; the presence of Jesus Christ in the consecrated bread and wine is a matter of faith. Faith based on the promise of Jesus himself.

How can this man give us his flesh to eat? A good question. The obvious question. And that was the very question raised when Jesus said that he would give us his flesh to eat.

Did Jesus back down from what he said? No way. In fact, he repeated his promise six times, in slightly different ways. Let us listen again to his words which we heard in today's Gospel:

- If you do not eat the flesh of the Son of Man and drink his blood, you will not have eternal life in you.
- Anyone who does eat my flesh and drink my blood has eternal life, and I shall raise that person up on the last day.

- For my flesh is real food and my blood is real drink.
- Whoever eats my flesh and drinks my blood lives in me and I live in that person.
- As the living Father sent me and I draw life from the Father, so whoever eats me will draw life from me.

Did Jesus want his words to be taken merely in a symbolic or metaphorical way, as if to say, 'I will be like bread and wine for you?'

No! Jesus meant what he said literally. When the people there did not accept what he said, they turned and walked away. He let them go. He did not call them back to say that he did not mean his words literally. 'Come back ... I did not mean those words literally about my flesh and blood.'

No! He did not call them back.

If Jesus did not intend the literal meaning of flesh and blood, then he was guilty of a major injustice to those who walked away.

How can this man give us his flesh to eat and his blood to drink? God had prepared the people for the miracle of his presence under the appearances of bread and wine.

In the Old Testament, we read how God fed the people with the mana from heaven. This was described as a gift from God ... the food of angels ... containing every delight, satisfying every taste ... transforming itself into what each eater wished (Wisdom 16:20-21)

Another preparation for the Eucharist was the bread provided for the prophet Elijah. On the strength of this bread he walked for forty days until he reached the holy mountain where he encountered God. The Eucharist is the bread of life

# The Real Presence

that gives us grace and support on our journey through life until we finally come face to face with God.

Jesus, in his ministry before the last supper, prepared the people by changing water into wine ... and by feeding thousands of people with a few loaves and fish. At the last supper he took the bread, blessed it, broke it and gave it to the disciples saying, 'This is my body'. He did the same with the cup of wine and said to them, 'This is my blood.'

Some twenty-five years after the last supper Saint Paul wrote the words we heard in today's Second Reading: 'The blessing cup that we bless is a communion with the blood of Christ, and the bread that we break is a communion with the body of Christ.' It is in all of the sacred scripture that we find the foundation of our beliefs in the Lord's presence in the Blessed Eucharist.

We speak of the real presence of Jesus in the Most Blessed Sacrament. This is not meant to suggest that there is anything unreal or untrue about the presence of the Lord in other ways ... such as the divine presence in Scripture which we call the word of God or the Lord's presence in the Christian community ... or the presence of Christ in works of charity or in moments of intimate prayer. But the presence of the Lord in the Blessed Sacrament is extra special. To quote the words of Pope Paul VI: 'It is a presence in the fullest sense: a substantial presence whereby Christ, the God-man, is wholly and entirely present.'

Because of our belief in this real, substantial presence, Catholics continue to reverence the Lord in the sacred hosts which have not been consumed during Mass. These consecrated hosts are not discarded. They are placed with reverence in the tabernacle. We genuflect before the Lord here present and maintain a light in the sanctuary lamp as a reminder of the divine presence. We seek the blessing of the Lord in Benediction of the Blessed Sacrament. We come in adoration before the Lord in the tabernacle. This is not idol worship, but a recognition of the Lord's presence. Somebody composed a little verse to express this faith:

> Whenever I pass by a church I make a little visit,
> Lest when I die and am brought in, the Lord should say, 'Who is it?'

St John Mary Vianney was deeply impressed by the faith of one of his parishioners who spent a long time in prayer before the tabernacle each day. What was he saying? What was he doing? His answer was: 'I look at him and he looks at me.' Lovers do not need words.

## Nineteenth Sunday in Ordinary Time: Year A

# Be Not Afraid

*Eamon Graham, Parish of Our Lady of Lourdes, Derry*

*Elijah finds God in the gentle breeze. Peter confesses Jesus to be the Son of God after the storm on the lake. During the storm Jesus tells the disciples, be not afraid. The mysterious presence of Christ is encountered in the Eucharist. These readings are read on 19th Sunday in Ordinary Time, Year A.*

We live in a world where so much is measured in terms of power and might, achievement and attainment, success and satisfaction.

The value of a country is measured in terms of its military and economic might. The value of a person is measured in terms of achievement, economic productivity and influence.

In today's first reading from the Book of Kings, one of the most beautiful of the Old Testament readings, we have the call of Elijah. Elijah does not find the call of God in the mighty wind; he does not find Him in the earthquake or the fire. He finds him in the gentle breeze.

# At the Breaking of Bread

The gentle breeze in our modern world is, in many ways, a counterbalance to the force and pressure in which we live our lives. It is found in ordinary people living ordinary lives.

Who are these ordinary people? They are you and I. Everyone is ordinary most of the time. Even the most famous and powerful may have their years of limelight and influence but behind all that they are just like you and me.

We all have to deal with disappointment and loss. Pain and suffering are part and parcel of our lives. For some of us they are publicly borne and obvious to those around us, especially in the case of sickness.

However, a lot of pain and suffering is hidden ... it is the pain of living, the sacrifices that we make in trying to follow Christ and in giving of ourselves to others. I think particularly of parents who sacrifice so much for their children, someone trying to care for sick relatives, someone trying to live in charity with the consequences of a broken relationship.

In today's Gospel Jesus calls us to step out into the unknown, to step out onto the water. The marvellous words of Jesus were the words that the late Pope John Paul used at the beginning of his pontificate ... 'Be not afraid'.

Jesus is with us on our journey. His sacrifice is ours. His Body and Blood are our nourishment. He will ask us the question that he asked the disciples on the road to Emmaus, 'Why are your faces downcast?' We will always recognise him in the breaking of the bread.

'Be not afraid.'

# CHRISTMAS

# CHRIST-MASS

*Tom Clancy PP, Parish of the Holy Spirit, Dennehy's Cross, Cork*

*Christmas is a time of extraordinary love and generosity of God coming among us, the Son of God, the Word made flesh. We observe Christmas through participation at Mass. The very word reminds us of that. But every day, every Sunday can be Christmas for those who believe in Christ's fruitful presence in the Eucharist.*

Christmas is an opportunity to underline the importance of the Eucharist, Christ's continued presence among us in Word and in the sign of bread and wine, consecrated and shared.

Have you been surprised yet this Christmas season? Has some member of the family arrived home unexpectedly? Or has some old friend or relation made contact after years of silence? Or has a neighbour surprised you with a thank you gift or invitation? I hope you enjoy some pleasant ongoing surprises today.

Surprises form the cornerstone of the Christmas Season. Certainly, the arrival of the Son of God as members of the human family took the whole world by surprise and continues to do so: so much so that many people who celebrate at Christmas do not realise the awesome wonder of what happened at Bethlehem and what continues to be celebrated on the birthday of Jesus. The contemporaries of Jesus expected a charismatic leader, a saviour of some sort, but what actually happened was so extraordinary that they refused to really take it on board. We can be like them in so many ways, but we have been given an insight into the mystery of a God who loves so totally that he gives himself to those he loves by sharing their human nature. The Christmas surprise is not only that Jesus was born of Mary, but that, in turn, we share in the divine life of God himself. We are adopted siblings of Jesus Christ, our Saviour. We are blessed to believe this and to nurture it in prayer.

We believe – Lord, help the little faith we have.

The other Christmas surprise is that the total giving of our Christmas God evokes such extraordinary love and generosity among true believers. Worldwide, at home and abroad, millions choose the Jesus option. They choose to make room at the inn of their hearts and their homes for the needy and the incapacitated, for the outcast and the rejected, for those without hope or home. They are instruments of reconciliation and peace reaching out across hostile unchartered relationships.

The power of example is irresistible. The spirit of Jesus enables us to imitate his example beyond our wildest dreams. His expectations for us are to imitate his style. The real surprise for us and for the world is when we do just that and continue to do so throughout the year. The wonder of these surprises need never fade. Jesus, Son of God, born of Mary, continues among us in his great gift of Himself in the Eucharist. It is this gift that challenges us and enables us to continue to make his presence effective in our world today.

It is a doubly creative gift. 'No one has ever seen God; it is the only Son who is nearest the Father's heart who had made him known' (John 1:18), primarily through the gift of the Eucharist. In turn, this gift moulds us to live through love in his presence with him as our everyday companion on life's journey. Through us, the Word continues to be made flesh. In God's plan, every day is Christmas Day for those willing to be surprised by the momentous arrival of the Son of God as Word made Flesh and by his ongoing fruitful presence in our Eucharist.

May the Lord continue to surprise you every day with his presence and love.

# WORD AND SACRIFICE

# Twentieth Sunday in Ordinary Time: Year C

## Servant of the Word

*John Watts PP, Holy Innocents Church, Southwark*

*Each follower of Christ has a prophetic vocation, that is, to be a servant of the Word of God. At Mass, the Word proclaimed is always a living active word. This homily was given on the 20th Sunday in Ordinary Time, Year C.*

At the Baptism Liturgy the anointing with oil of chrism is accompanied with the following prayer, 'As Christ was anointed priest, prophet and king so may you live always as a member of his body, sharing everlasting life.' It is strange how the word 'prophet' has changed its meaning over time. Originally meaning a spokesperson, it is now associated with telling the future, whether or not I will win this week's lottery! The Word of God takes us back to that original meaning.

The Prophet Jeremiah lived at a time of uncertainty and political weakness. Our first reading shows the difficulties and uncertainties he is facing. He is saved from death by the intervention of Ebed-melech, the Cushite. What the passage reveals to us is the demands of the prophetic vocation. It is not always easy or acceptable to be God's spokesperson. Not everyone is waiting on tenterhooks for the message that the prophet will bring. A prophet's vocation is a servant vocation, a servant of the Word of God. This is the Word, which has to be preached 'in and out of the season'.

In the ordination liturgies of both priests and deacons the following is said, 'Believe what you read, teach what you believe, practise what you teach.' Today's Gospel is in contrast to so much of what we preach about Jesus. It is a reading that makes us feel uncomfortable. Possibly we do not want to hear that the Gospel will bring about division, especially in our own family circles. There cannot be a neutral position on the teaching of Jesus; it will always challenge us to go a step further, to walk into the unknown. But all of us, through our baptism, have this Gospel placed in our hands. Like the ordained we too are asked to read, teach and practise it. This is how we fulfil our sharing in the prophetic ministry of Jesus, how we grow into being servants of the Word.

As we consider the life and ministry of Jesus we find many instances where he was rejected and misunderstood. Initially his very background is the reason why some refuse to accept him while others rejected 'his deplorable language' and walked no longer with him. When a rich young man, who genuinely wants to enter the kingdom, is told that he must give away all he has, it is a demand so great he rejects it and walks away.

How well do we live at our prophetic calling in daily life? Are we servants to the Gospel in our actions as well as in our words? It is easy to list the grand events on the international stage where a prophetic voice is needed, for example, to speak out against racism or exploitation, to highlight the plight of the poor and downcast. In the Letter for the Year of the Eucharist,

*Mane nobiscum Domine*, the late Pope John Paul II asked us 'to commit (ourselves) in a particular way to responding with fraternal solicitude to one of the many forms of poverty present in or our world' (28). These are times when the Church, the community of faith, fulfils her role as prophet, servant of the Word. But a similar strength and courage is needed in our personal lives to say that using the office's franking machine of personal post is stealing or challenging the belief that putting down extra expenses is our right!

If all this seems so demanding and beyond us then let us be consoled by the second reading today by the 'many witnesses' who 'did not lose sight of Jesus'. They are not just Oscar Romeros or Edith Steins, but ordinary people like you or me who were faithful to the Gospel given to them, who 'practised what they preached' and thereby lived fully their sharing in the prophetic ministry of Jesus and became servants of the Word.

# Nineteenth Sunday in Ordinary Time: Year B

# On Understanding Sacrifice

*Eamon Graham, Parish of Our Lady of Lourdes, Derry*

*Biblical stories and human experience inform us of the meaning of sacrifice, a concept intimately part of our Eucharistic faith. In the Gospel, John 6:41-45, read on 19th Sunday in Ordinary Time, Year B, Jesus tells us that he is the Bread of Life, the living bread, given for the life of the world.*

I remember in my early years of priesthood receiving a phone call from the police to say that a young man from the parish had died tragically in England. It was late on a New Year's night, almost midnight. Because of the ongoing violence in Derry at the time, the police did not respond to such calls and it was my task to inform the family.

I remember almost feeling deceitful in going to the door of his mother's house; she was elderly, sick and lived alone. I was warmly welcomed, brought in and we sat down.

I broke the news and after about five minutes of silence the old lady looked at me and said, 'Thanks be to God for our priests. What would we do without them?' I had a great feeling of inadequacy and unworthiness of a comment like that ... yet I soon realised that it was God that she was talking about and not me.

In trying to live the Christian life sacrifice is to be expected. We can be married, single, religious or a priest. All of these vocations demand a dying to self. In the 1970s there was a craze for 'Argus posters'. Every self-respecting student had a dozen or so on the wall. One particular one stands out in my mind. The quote was 'We should always be prepared at any time to sacrifice what we are for what we could become'. I think that this sums up the Christian life but it will always involve pain and sacrifice.

Elijah in the first reading was fed up. He had had enough and he wanted to journey no more, just to sleep. Cannot we identify so much with these feelings? We are all tempted at times to stop trying to live the Christian life. We can so easily say, 'Look at those who don't bother. They seem to be quite happy.' The temptation is to lie down and rest, to immerse ourselves in a material world and forget that our journey is an eternal one.

In small ways we are used to making sacrifices for material gain. We spend hours in study to pass exams and to gain employment. We save money in order to purchase the things of life, we save for holidays.

We are asked to make sacrifices for our eternal journey. The route of that journey is not all that important but the destination is. The angel left Elijah with bread for the journey.

St John tells us that the Eucharist is our bread for eternal life; the food for our journey. In the simplicity of the bread and wine the sacrifice of Jesus on Calvary and that of lives become one, we travel forwards together:

## At the Breaking of Bread

Anyone who eats the bread will live forever and the Bread that I shall give is My Flesh for the life of the world.

## NINETEENTH SUNDAY IN ORDINARY TIME: YEAR B

# EMBRACING SACRIFICE

*Eamon Graham, Parish of Our Lady of Lourdes, Derry*

*We embrace sacrifice in our Christian living, in human experience, in understanding the meaning of the death and resurrection of Christ and in the Eucharist, the sacrifice of the Mass. The Gospel reading, Luke 12:32-48 is read on 19th Sunday in Ordinary Time, Year A. Its advice that we must stand ready is also a theme for Advent and the month of November.*

The past one hundred years have seen breathtaking advances in terms of scientific discovery and human advancement. I am often fascinated in looking at old photographs in houses of gathers of people, especially in rural Ireland, particularly those taken in the early decades of the last century. I am especially amazed when an older person points to an individual child in the photograph and proudly identifies herself. The child, like the rest of the children, is barefoot. It was commonplace to travel barefoot to school from May to October. It shows how much Ireland has changed.

While it is easy to look back nostalgically to simpler, more wholesome times, the truth is that every age has its good and bad points. Accepted values and norms in society may fluctuate but the balance of goodness is always there.

In past times, when life was materially one of struggle and sacrifice, it was a great comfort to accept the fact that life was passing and the next life was something to look forward to.

We in the west no longer walk to school in our bare feet; we do not wonder where the next meal will come from; we no longer hope for an apple and an orange in our Christmas stocking. In our life of plenty and of relative luxury, we can begin to believe that we will live forever.

We are obsessed with fitness, with diets, with appearance and image. We forget that life passes for us all – it is the only certainty that we have. It is reassuring to see the traditions of the wake continuing as it makes death real for us all, especially those of the younger generation.

Today's readings talk about the things that we cannot see, the things that demand our faith. At the beginning, I talked of the Ireland of the past: it had its pluses and minuses, people had difficult lives and made many sacrifices, but were sustained by a deep faith in God and the things of God. Perhaps it was necessary for survival but it was there nevertheless and was very important.

The Gospel calls us to be ready for the arrival of the master whenever that might be. This in one way seems stark but is nevertheless vital for Christian living. If we wish to embrace the Sermon on the Mount as a pattern for Christian living then we must also embrace the Passion and Resurrection of Jesus.

St Francis used to refer to Sister Death. If we look at ourselves in terms of eternity then death can become a friend, not one we want to embrace immediately, but one we can happily embrace at the appropriate time.

We can train for this meeting by embracing the sacrifices that everyday Christian living requires. This embrace is found in the deepest possible way in the Sacrifice of the Mass when we meet the Communion of Saints, both the living and the dead.

> You must stand ready because the Son of Man is coming at an hour that you don't expect.

Let us greet him as a friend.

# BREAD OF LIFE, CUP OF SALVATION

## Twenty-Eighth Sunday in Ordinary Time: Year A

# An Invitation to the Feast

*Tony Flannery CSsR, Esker, Athenry, Co. Galway*

*The Mass is our great prayer of thanksgiving. Sunday after Sunday we are invited to the feast, 'a banquet of rich food,' to use the phrase of Isaiah 25:6. The reading Isaiah 25:6-10 is read with the Gospel story of the king who gave a feast for his son's wedding (Matthew 22:1-14) on 28th Sunday in Ordinary Time, Year A. The reading from Isaiah is read on Wednesday, 1st Week of Advent and on All Souls Day. It is a reading often chosen at funerals where it reminds us that Eucharist on earth is fulfilled in the banquet of heaven.*

I remember when I was a teenager complaining to my mother that I was bored at Mass, and didn't get anything out of it. The answer she gave didn't mean much to me at the time, but later I remembered it and could see its wisdom. What she said was: 'Our Mass is as good as our lives'.

The people invited to the wedding feast in today's Gospel didn't want to go because they had other things in their lives that they regarded as more important. The farm and the business needed attention. We too can get lost in a lifestyle that is detrimental to what happens at the Eucharist.

When I think of my mother's sentence I can see that the fundamental meaning of the Mass involves four attitudes that are also important in life.

It is possible for us to meet Christ at Mass. But it doesn't happen automatically. In order to meet Christ we need a heightened awareness, sensitivity, an ability to live in the present. Unless we have these attitudes, unless we are already aware of the presence of Christ in the ordinariness of our daily life, it is unlikely that we will meet Him in the Eucharist in any real of meaningful way.

The Mass is a communal celebration, a sharing of life and faith. We come to it with a community of believers. But unless we are in the habit of sharing, unless we are generous of ourselves, our time and our possessions in our ordinary life, it is unlikely that we will be able to fully participate in the community aspect of the Mass.

The Mass is the great prayer of thanksgiving. But an attitude of thankfulness is not something that can be switched on when we enter the door of the church. It involves a deep appreciation of life, of the gifts of God, and of the people around us. If we are in the habit of thanking God and the people with whom we live each day, then we will bring that spirit to Mass and it will find its deepest expression there.

The Mass is an offering. We offer ourselves, all that we have and are, with the offering of Christ in the Eucharist. But in order to do that with any conviction we need to have a solid appreciation of ourselves and our worth as people. We must believe that we are worth offering.

## An Invitation to the Feast

If we haven't developed these values and attitudes in our lives then, like the people in the Gospel, we are also likely to refuse the invitation. We will be too busy with other things. But if our lives are imbued with them we will want to be at the feast. In the first reading Isaiah gives a marvellous description of that feast. The Lord will prepare a banquet of rich food, of fine wines. He will destroy death and wipe away every tear. We will be happy and glad to accept the invitation.

Thank you, Lord, for your invitation to the wedding feast. It is our privilege to attend.

Eighteenth Sunday in Ordinary Time: Year A

# They Collected the Scraps

Frank Murray PP, Ferbane, Co. Offaly

*The scraps that fall from the rich man's table are mentioned on a few occasions in the Gospels but the Gospel story of the feeding of the five thousand (Matthew 14:13-21), read on the 18th Sunday in Ordinary Time, Year A (and on Monday after this Sunday when this Gospel is not the Sunday Gospel), tells us that what was left over was collected 'after all ate as much as they wanted.' The story is also told in John 6:1-15 on 17th Sunday in Ordinary Time, Year B and in Luke 9:11-17 on the Solemnity of the Body and Blood of Christ (Corpus Christi), Year C. Mark's account (6:34-44) is the Gospel for 8 January.*

'They collected the scraps, remaining...'

After the miracle of the loaves and fishes, 'they collected the scraps'. This phrase has always intrigued me. It has echoes of the story of Lazarus, waiting hungrily for the scraps that fall

## They Collected the Scraps

from the rich man's table (Luke 16:21). The Syrophoenician woman said to Jesus that even the dogs could eat the scraps that fell from the table (Mark 4:29). 'Scraps' seems to be a Gospel word.

We have 'scrap yards' and 'scrap heaps' that speak to us of things and people that the world considers obsolete. Gathering up the scraps speaks to us of the care of food and the sacredness of bread. It speaks to us of a world of excess and waste side by side with a world of famine and malnutrition.

> Be gentle when you touch bread.
> Let it not be
> Uncared for – unwanted.
> There is so much beauty in the bread.
> Beauty of the sun and soil,
> Beaut of the patient toil.
> Winds and rain have caressed it,
> Christ often blessed it.
> Be gentle
> When you touch bread.
> *Anonymous*

In this context I like to think of the 'Gospel scraps' as the every day experience of grace that we often fail to collect, because we are too busy. We don't see. We don't wake up to smell the coffee, or anything else for that matter, during the day. We miss the scraps, because, as Patrick Kavanagh said in *The Great Hunger*, we dream of…

## At the Breaking of Bread

>The absolute envased banquet
>all or nothing. And it was nothing.
>For God is not all in one place, complete...

And so there is a great hunger for meaning and mystery and the grace of god in the bits and pieces, the scraps of everyday experience. These scraps are like the grains of golden corn, strewn in the rich soil of our hearts, which we garner to make and bake the daily bread of the Eucharist. Often we come to the Lord of Sunday with empty baskets and empty hearts... we have neglected to collect the scraps of the ordinary, that makes sense of God. We have no bread or fish to offer the Lord to transform into our 'Bread of Life'.

>Gather and garner the golden grain
>The scattered seeds of plenty,
>The scraps of everyday bread
>Strewn on the pathway of my life.
>
>My heart is like an empty basket
>Turned completely upside-down,
>Stretching and straining with anxious hands
>To grasp the gracious gift of grain.
>
>It simply rolls down the side,
>Wasted in arid soil of forgotten memories
>Of taste and touch and sight and smell,
>Leaving me with no crumb of comfort.
>
>Lord, take me in your healing hands,
>When evening falls in a lonely place

# They Collected the Scraps

Turn me right side-up again
To basket the scraps with open heart.

Bless me with the gift of common sense
Of sight and smell and touch and taste,
That I may garner every grain of truth
As seeds of love and thanks – Your Holy Eucharist.

## SEVENTEENTH SUNDAY IN ORDINARY TIME: YEAR A

# PEARL OF GREAT PRICE

*Ken O'Riordan,*
*Adult Education Adviser for the Diocese of Nottingham*

*Communion is a word in a number of different phrases. It is the Communion of the Eucharistic Body and Blood of Christ. There is the communion with others and there is the communion of saints. Communion is a pearl of great price. The phrase, pearl of great price, is taken from Matthew 13:44-52, the Gospel of 17th Sunday in Ordinary Time, Year A.*

In 1990 I was working for a few months in Western Australia and was about to take a flight to the Northern Part of the country. I hadn't phoned home since I arrived and just took the time to make the call: 'Darby isn't very well and we're waiting for the doctor to come' was the news I received. 'Do you want to talk to him? He's down in the room?' 'I'm fine' my father said to me, but the tone and the obvious pain in the voice told a very different story. As I put down the phone it was as if I had already left Western Australia. My Australian hosts were very kind and helpful in cancelling the rest of my engagements and arranging for a flight back home. I arrived at the hospital the following evening to see my father in a state of deep unconsciousness and pain. When I reached the bed side he came up out of the unconscious and said the following; 'So you flew into Farranfore [Kerry Airport]! That's good.' Then he slipped back into an unsettled unconsciousness.

It was a very strange moment full of a great mixture of emotions. At its heart it was a moment of true communion, becoming one together and at the same time questions just flowed through my mind: Should I have accepted the invitation to go to Australia? Should I have stayed at home? He'd seemed so well a few weeks ago just before I left, how had I failed to see how bad he really was? A year later my cousin, who had known just how bad he'd been told me that she had decided not to tell me as she knew that I wouldn't have gone if I'd known. And that my father was so proud of my being invited to go. I treasured that conversation – it was a pearl of great price.

When I was thinking about the Gospel of today's Mass with its rich imagery, treasure, pearl of great price, sorting out which fish to keep and which to throw away, taking out of the storeroom things both new and old, the moment which I've shared kept coming into my mind. For me it holds the clarity and complexity of recognising the true treasure and the pearl of great price – the realisation of just how necessary it is to make a judgement and not know whether that judgement is right or wrong while all the time listening to your deepest truth, trusting that all will be well. The parables in the Gospel are more like riddles and riddles are an invitation to engage with the possibilities offered.

Personally I love the image of taking out of the storeroom things both new and old. The joy and shock of what was kept by my parents when we finally came to sort out the house after both had died, the old photographs in a cardboard box, images of us as children, treasured and kept, not thrown out, each one a pearl. The difficulty for us, trying to decide which to keep and which to let go! The fact that not one of us could take down our mother's coat from the back of the door for five years! All of which holds something of the mystery, in which we live and move and have our being.

An insight into the communion of saints, I still keep my mother's prayer book with all its bits and pieces. Just the feel and smell of it keeps me in touch with the mystery and in the words of the poet Brendan Kennelly, 'I know that it does not matter that I do not understand.'

BODY AND BLOOD OF CHRIST (CORPUS CHRISTI): YEAR B

# THE BLOOD OF THE NEW COVENANT

*Silvester O'Flynn OFMCap., Holy Trinity, Mathew Quay, Cork*

> At Mass when the wine is taken, the priest recalls the night before Jesus died. On that night he took the bread and wine and blessed them. The wine 'is my blood, the blood of the covenant, poured out...' The Gospel for the feast of the Body and Blood of Christ (Corpus Christi), Year B is Matthew's account of the institution of the Eucharist. The first reading, Exodus 24:3-8, helps us to understand the significance of 'the blood of the new covenant.' The second reading, Hebrews 9:11-15, reminds us that this is the perfect sacrifice, 'once and for all'.

'This is my blood, the blood of the covenant, which is to be poured out for you.'

The Feast of the Body and Blood of Christ, Corpus Christi, is a celebration of the presence of Jesus Christ in the Blessed Eucharist. There are many different themes associated with the Eucharist which might be developed: the real presence, the

Eucharist and the life of the Church, the Eucharist of sacrifice, the Eucharist as meal, the dispositions of mind and heart before receiving Eucharist, the obligations on those who receive the Lord to pass on his love and so on. Today we will follow the theme of the blood of the new covenant since the three readings of today's liturgy are about covenant and blood.

What is meant by the covenant? A covenant is an agreement made between parties, with obligations on both sides. In religious terms, the covenant refers to the relationship established between God and his people. The entire bible may be seen as the story of two covenants. That is why we refer to it as a book of two testaments: the Old Testament composed of writings about the covenant between God and the people before the time of Christ; and the New Testament composed of writings about the new life offered by Jesus Christ to people.

The old covenant, sometimes called the first covenant, developed in three stages. First, God made a covenant with Noah after the flood. God promised never to destroy the earth again: and the people's part of the bargain was to end murder and the destruction of life.

The second stage of the covenant was with Abraham. Abraham accepted the position of Yahweh as the one and only God. In return, he was given the promise of a great line of descendants.

The old covenant was completed with Moses. God led the people out of the slavery of Egypt and promised the people that they would be his chosen people. Their part was to observe the commandments. The First Reading of today's Mass describes the sacrifice of animals to mark the ratification of the covenant. The seal was put on the promises, not with ink, not with wax, but with blood. One might still see that custom in films about the Mafia. If two Mafia bosses make a pact, it is ratified by nicking a small cut in their hands or wrists and clamping the two together. A covenant sealed with blood meant that the price would be one's life. If one party breaks the agreement, the other is entitled to take the life of the betrayer. When the covenant was ratified with a blood sacrifice it indicated that this was a matter of life and death.

In Old Testament times there were multiple sacrifices of animals. Today's Second Reading, from the Letter to the Hebrews, takes up this idea of the repeated sacrifices. The writer rejoices that the one sacrifice of Jesus Christ, shedding his blood on the cross, has replaced all those animal sacrifices. The sacrifice of Jesus was perfect. In his sacrificial death he inaugurated the new covenant: the new life that would be gifted to the disciples in the coming of the Holy Spirit. Unlike the sacrifices of the Old Testament when each sacrifice needed new animals for the slaughter, with Jesus the one act of sacrifice is perfect and does not need to be repeated.

But, you might ask, what about the Mass? Do we repeat the death of Jesus in every Mass? Does Jesus die in every Mass? Of course not. Jesus died just once, on one day in history on the hill of Calvary.

So, what happens at mass? Let us quote from the *Catechism of the Catholic Church:*

> Christian liturgy not only recalls the events that saved us but actualises them, makes them present. The Paschal mystery of Christ is celebrated, not repeated. It is the celebrations that are repeated and in each celebration there is an outpouring of

the Holy Spirit that makes the unique mystery present (1104).

All other historical events happened just once and were swallowed up in the past. But the sacrificial death of Jesus destroyed death. Hence, his death and resurrection participate in the divine eternity. Every time we celebrate the Eucharist we are celebrating the journey of Christ through death in returning to the Father. The sacrificial outpouring of the blood of Jesus is not repeated. It is our celebration which is repeated. Saint Paul told the Corinthians: 'Until the Lord comes, therefore, every time you eat this bread and drink this cup, you are proclaiming his death.' (1 Cor 11:26)

Today's Gospel from Saint Mark takes us back to the evening when Jesus celebrated the Passover with his disciples. At the Passover they were celebrating the deliverance of the Israelites from the slavery of Egypt. On the night of their deliverance the destroying angel passed through the land of Egypt but passed over the dwellings of the Israelites which were marked by the sprinkled blood of a lamb that had been sacrificed. They were saved by the blood of a lamb.

Jesus was about to offer up his life in sacrifice to deliver the whole world from the slavery of sin. At the supper he anticipated his sacrificial death in a ritual. Taking some bread, he said the blessing, broke it and gave it to them saying, 'This is my body'. He did the same with the cup, saying to them: 'This is my blood, the blood of the covenant, which is to be poured out for many.'

'This is my body.' That means this is the gift of myself to you. In English when we speak of everybody, somebody or anybody, we are not referring to bodies like corpses. We mean every person, some person, any person. Body here means person, the unique, identifiable package of life that is me. Jesus, in saying 'this is my body', is saying, 'this is my presence in person to you.'

And in saying, 'this is my blood, the blood of the covenant', he is saying, 'this is I who unite you with the Father through the blood shed to ratify the new covenant'. Jesus is the true Lamb of God whose blood shed in sacrifice takes away the sins of the world.

The relationship set up in this new covenant is nothing less than the invitation to become children of God, one with Christ in sharing the divine life. The sustenance of this divine life has to be a divine food. It is nothing less than Jesus himself, truly present in the consecrated bread and wine. By this divine food we deepen our union with God and grow in the likeness of Christ. As Saint Augustine so beautifully explained, this divine food is not digested as ordinary food to become part of us, but by it we are changed to become more truly part of Christ.

The Feast of Corpus Christi is an occasion to renew our faith in the presence of the Lord Jesus under the signs of the bread and wine.

'This is my body', he said. This is Jesus, really and truly present.

'This is my blood, the blood of the covenant, which is to be poured out for you.'

This is Jesus whose shedding of blood is the perfect sacrifice, taking away all sin and ratifying the new covenant, under which we are given the power to become the children of God.

Seventeenth Sunday in Ordinary Time: Year C

# Communion, Our Peace

*Ken O'Riordan,*
*Adult Education Adviser for the Diocese of Nottingham*

*Our preparation for Communion includes the Lord's Prayer and the sign of peace. The bread we pray for in the Lord's Prayer includes the Eucharistic Bread and the peace we exchange with one another finds its deepest expression in Eucharistic Communion. St Luke's account of some of the teaching of Christ in the Gospel read on 17th Sunday in Ordinary Time, Year C includes the Lord's Prayer and a teaching on the prayer of petition, 'Ask, and it shall be given to you.' St Matthew also has the Lord's Prayer and the same prayer of petition (6:9-13), the Gospel reading of Tuesday, 1st Week in Lent and Thursday, 11th Week in Ordinary Time.*

A conversation I had with a friend of mine a few years ago came to mind as I watched the funeral mass of Pope John Paul II, 'I don't mind going to Mass but I can't stand the sign of peace. Every time I go I look around to see who's there and then I decide where to sit so I can avoid the sign of peace as much as possible.' The close proximity of Mr Mugabe, President of Zimbabwe, to Prince Charles along with the leaders from Iran and Iraq, Syria and Israel was striking. None of these would normally extend the hand of friendship to one another, yet they did so at the sign of peace, regardless of the backlash they might receive when they returned home. It was simply the right thing to do.

That sign of peace showed, however fleetingly, the possibilities that are always present if we approach one another through the eyes of friendship rather than through the eyes of suspicion and mistrust. In fact every hand extended in friendship is a reflection of the inner life of the Trinity and is captured in the opening phrase of the prayer Jesus offered his disciples in today's liturgy. 'Our Father'. Not 'My Father' but *Our* Father and the 'our' is in no way exclusive, it doesn't refer simply to Catholics or Christians of other persuasions but to All, regardless of race, religion or culture. It is why in one of the older forms of introduction to the prayer the words 'we dare to say' are used. Dare we believe that God is Father, no exceptions, because if we did just how rich and at the same time how vulnerable we would make ourselves in our relations with one another?

It is perhaps why the Gospel today invites us to ask, search, knock and find. And we will be given the gift of the Holy Spirit. The answer to all prayer seems to be the gift of the Holy Spirit rather than the more superficial 'getting what I want'. As Oscar Wilde once put it, 'When the gods want to punish us they answer our prayers'. I know that a lot of my own prayer is really a kind of wish list rather than a deep desire to be transformed. For many years I was bedevilled by a spirituality of 'offering up' or 'putting up with' things that couldn't be changed rather than a spirituality which seeks to transform or give new meaning to whatever happens. The answer to all prayer is the Holy Spirit – from 'Let me win the Lottery (and I'll give lots away to charity)' to praying for someone who is seriously ill or in a situation of deep unresolved hurt, the answer always lies in a deep desire to receive the Holy Spirit.

The great story in which Fionn of the Fianna answers the question, 'Which is the greatest sound of all?' with the answer that the greatest sound of all is the, 'Music of what Happens', is shot through with the gift of the Holy Spirit and the more contemporary reflections of the poet Brendan Kennelly also carry this gift:

> For such things
> And bearing in mind
> The midnight hurt, the shot bride,
> The famine in the heart,
> The demented soldier, the terrified cities
> Rising out of their own rubble,
> I give thanks.
>   (A Giving)

It is this deep desire to transform which lies at the heart of every mass, of every hand extended in friendship. The desire to give thanks no matter what and no matter how difficult.

The sign of peace is a recognition that we are all children of the One Father, that we are all called to give thanks, in fact to give Eucharist to one another.

SERVICE

# Holy Thursday

# Eucharist – A Life of Service

*Dermot Lane PP, Balally, Dublin*

*A Eucharistic people cannot be indifferent to injustice and inequality. Each celebration of Mass, therefore, challenges us to a life of service of others. The Gospel story of the washing of the feet of the disciples, read on Holy Thursday's Evening Mass of the Lord's Supper is a powerful reminder of this perspective.*

Anything you do on a regular basis runs the risk of becoming routine, mechanical, and ultimately boring. This is a principle that applies right across the broad spectrum of human activity. It also applies to the way we celebrate the Eucharist, Sunday after Sunday. We are all creatures of habit, and we constantly need to review our habits lest we get into a rut.

Holy Thursday gives us a moment to review the way we celebrate the Eucharist, an opportunity to renew our faith in the Eucharist, and an occasion to deepen our understanding of Christ's gift to the church.

For all of us, the Eucharist is at the centre of Christian faith, the source of unity binding us together as a people, as a parish and as a church. The Eucharist is also food for the journey of life and a living memorial of the life, death and Resurrection of Jesus.

These are some of the features of the Eucharist that support us as a Christian people. There are, however, other aspects of the Eucharist that challenge the imagination, namely the link between the Eucharist and solidarity with others, the connection between the celebration of Mass and the service of others, the relationship between the Eucharist and the work of justice.

It is these disturbing and prophetic dimensions of the Eucharist that come to mind this evening as we celebrate Holy Thursday.

Holy Thursday is about the institution of the Eucharist at the Last Supper by Jesus. Our second reading reminds us of how Jesus, on the night he was betrayed, took bread, thanked God, and broke the bread saying, 'This is my body...' Our Gospel reading, taken from St John, gives us not an institution narrative as the other three other Gospels do, but rather an account of the washing of the feet that took place immediately after the institution of the Eucharist. There are at least two points that should be noted about the institution of the Eucharist.

(1) As we all know, the Eucharist was instituted at the Last Supper, that particular supper which comes at the end of a series of suppers throughout the life of Jesus. If you read the Gospels, you will be struck, indeed amazed, at the number of times Jesus celebrated meals with people and the number of occasions in which he enters into a new type of table-fellowship with all kinds of characters. A distinctive feature of this meal ministry in the life of Jesus is that it is inclusive, indeed so

inclusive that the scribes and Pharisees complained and said: 'Look, a glutton and a drunkard, a friend of tax collectors and sinners' (Matthew 11:19). It is not nice to be called a glutton and a drunkard in any company! On the other hand, from a Jewish point of view, Jesus was cavorting with tax collectors and sinners who in that culture were regarded as ritually impure and therefore to be avoided.

The meals of Jesus, however, transcended these religious conventions and boundaries by embracing all and by being radically inclusive. The gift of the Eucharist from Christ to the Church is intended, in the light of the meal ministry of Jesus and the Last Supper, to be inclusive, to be available for all; the Eucharist is not therefore exclusive and not therefore just for an elite and not therefore only for religious people.

The celebration of the Eucharist in the life of the Church should be a zone of inclusivity, a place of equality, a moment of communion between rich and poor, insiders and outsiders, young and old.

The second point to note about Holy Thursday is the emphasis placed on the washing of the feet. This prophetic action by Jesus is a commentary on the deeper meaning of the Eucharist, a dramatic declaration which says that if you celebrate the Eucharist, then you must embrace a life of service. Commitment to Christ in the Eucharist carries with it a commitment to Christ in the poor, the needy and the marginalised within society.

We cannot be a Eucharistic people and at the same time be indifferent to the existence of injustices and inequalities within society. It is at this level that the Eucharist challenges us, indeed disturbs and provokes us, to be involved in a new life of service.

And so, to sum up, our celebration of Holy Thursday has two clear messages, that is, two important lessons for the way that we as a people celebrate Sunday Eucharist throughout the year: how can we ensure that our celebration of the Eucharist is inclusive, that there is room for everybody around the table of the Lord – tax collectors and sinners, insiders and outsiders, nationals and non-nationals alike?

If we dare to come together around the one table to re-enact the Last Supper, in the light of the death and resurrection of Christ, then we must be prepared to make a clear connection between the Eucharist and action for justice, between the celebration of the sacrificial Paschal Meal and a personal commitment to a new life of solidarity with others.

# Twentieth Sunday in Ordinary Time: Year A

## Eucharist leads to Service

*John Watts PP, Holy Innocents Church, Southwark*

*'I will be your God, you will be my people' (Ezekiel 36:28, as heard at the Easter Vigil) sums up the covenant between God and Israel. Yet it is always about salvation is for all and God's chosen people are called to serve. The readings for the 20th Sunday in Ordinary Time, Year A underline that salvation is for all and our participation in Eucharist urges us to service, especially in works of healing, peace and justice. The Gospel reading, Matthew 15:21-28, is also read on Wednesday, 18th week.*

The experience of being chosen is one which is familiar to all of us; it probably started when we were young in the school playground as the two captains called out the names of those they wanted for their respective teams. It reaches a high point for most of us when someone chooses us as the one they love and want to spend their life with. Being chosen is being considered special. Being chosen is a key theme in the Christian scriptures. The People of God in the Old Testament, the Israelites, were very conscious of the call they had received, a call from God. 'I will be your God, you will be my people.' That choice revealed to them that they were special in the eyes of God, chosen to find a new life in a promised land, chosen to be led from slavery to freedom.

But how quickly complacency and arrogance can creep into human existence and replace choice and uniqueness. How easy it is to forget one's simple origins and for familiarity to breed contempt. Sadly, the History of Salvation reveals how that happened to God's chosen people, how the Israelites after being led by God's protection and love to the safety of the Promised Land, literally lose their way once they have arrived. A reading of the religious history of Israelites shows a decline into sinfulness and a leaving of the path of holiness; their very calling is forgotten and rejection and exile replace choice and uniqueness. They have to learn a new lesson – salvation is for all and they will be servants. Choice leads to service.

In many ways the period of exile is a time of rude awakening to the realisation of what they had lost. It proved to be a long and painful road to restoration and then a new understanding of what it means to be chosen. Such a choice of the Israelites is not just for them but also for all. This is where our first reading from Isaiah begins, 'Foreigners... these I will bring to my holy mountain.' Salvation is not for the few but available to all and this is the service that the Israelites must give. By hearing the cries for justice and responding with integrity, they will be the servants, the instruments for others to be saved. But a new lesson takes time to sink into human consciousness.

A foreigner appears in the Gospel to reinforce the teaching of Isaiah. A simple request from an anguished and distressed woman fails to touch the hearts of the disciples, their response is 'give her what she wants. Get off our backs.' How do we interpret the silence of Jesus? However, it is the persistence of this woman that breaks the silence. Her faith brings the response of Jesus to her pleas and reveals him as 'the one who came to serve but not to be served.' Jesus' mission is one of service and reaching out to those crying for justice, for healing, for peace.

In Baptism we entered the community life of God, Father and Holy Spirit. Our communion with God is one, which grows through prayer and the sacraments. The deeper the communion becomes, the more we become aware of God's choice and our commitment to bringing his salvation to others. How will we do it? Today in the celebration of this Eucharist we realise the uniqueness of God's choice and are given an impulse 'for a practical commitment to building a more just and fraternal society'. (*Mane nobiscum Domine*, 28)

We need to hear the cries of the 'outsider' for justice and salvation. Jesus shows us how to respond. Gone is the triumphalism of the past for our Community of Faith, in its place is a servant Church in dialogue with all, listening and responding to the needs of all, conscious of being chosen and working towards the fulfilment of today's responsorial psalm 'that all the nations will learn your saving help'.

Body and Blood of Christ (Corpus Christi): Year C

## 'Give Them Something to Eat Yourselves'

*Silvester O'Flynn OFMCap, Holy Trinity, Mathew Quay, Cork*

*One phrase prompts several thoughts on the meaning of Communion, especially the responsibility to be agents of God's love for others. The word Communion reminds us of responsibility. At the end of Mass we are dismissed to go in peace and to love and serve the Lord. This phrase in the story of the feeding of the five thousand in St Luke's Gospel (read on the Solemnity of the Body and Blood of Christ (Corpus Christi), Year C) is also in St Matthew's version (read on 18th Sunday in Ordinary Time, Year A) and in St Mark's version (read on 8 January).*

'Give them something to eat yourselves.'
That is what Jesus said to the twelve apostles when they expressed concern about the hunger and lodgings of the vast crowd. The people are hungry and this is a lonely place.

# 'Give Them Something To Eat Yourselves'

'Give them something to eat yourselves.'
Jesus then in a wonderful miracle multiplied the bread and fishes to feed the multitude. But one very significant feature of the story is the extent to which he involved the apostles. He got them to organise the crowd. He told them to distribute the food. And he got them to gather up the leftovers in baskets, enough for twelve, one for each apostle. The miracle of the loaves and fishes prepared the minds of people to accept the miracle of the last supper when Jesus changed the bread and wine into his body and blood. The involvement of the apostles in the miracle of the loaves and fishes anticipated the obligations that rest on those who receive the Lord in the Eucharist to be active agents of the Lord's love in the world.

'Give them something to eat yourselves.'
For years I had understood that the word Communion originated in the word '*Unio*', meaning our personal union with Christ in the Eucharist. With this meaning in mind, the Eucharist is understood as a very intimate, personal union with the Lord. It opened my mind when I came to see that the letter 'm' occurs twice in the middle of communion. The word does not originate in '*unio*' but in '*munio*', meaning a burden or responsibility that I carry. Communion means more than a personal meeting with the Lord. Communion means a shared mission, sharing in the mission of Jesus Christ. That is why the last words of the Mass, after the Final Blessing, express our mission to go out, to love and serve the Lord. We are to move from Mass to mission. The Eucharistic banquet of Christ's self-giving love is completed only when we pass on Christ's love to others.

St John put it like this in his First Letter: 'No one has ever seen God, but as long as we love one another God remains in us and his love comes to perfection in us.' His love comes to perfection in us. Saint John is saying that God's love is incomplete until we pass it on. It is like electricity. The power does not get through if there is a break in the circuit. God's love is short-circuited if we do not pass it on.

'Give them something to eat yourselves.'
When we speak of the Real Presence of the Lord we are usually referring to the divine presence in the consecrated bread and wine. But the reality of Christ's presence in the Eucharist brings the challenge to let the reality of Christ's presence be seen in practical, everyday love.

One person whose life was inspired by this mission was Blessed Mother Teresa of Calcutta. She described the typical day of her sisters, the Missionaries of Christ like this, 'We begin each day by trying to see Christ through the Bread, and during the day we continue to see him hidden beneath the torn bodies of the poor.' Or again, she said, 'The Holy Hour before the Eucharist should lead us to the Holy Hour with the poor. Our Eucharist lacks something if it does not lead us to love and serve the poor.'

'Give them something to eat yourselves.'
The times we live in have seen people become too focused on themselves as individuals. One of the underlying sins of the twentieth century was an excessive focus on the individual with the loss of the sense of family and community. For many, religion has become a very private affair, a me-God relationship, lacking any sense of social belonging. It is about my salvation, about feeling cleansing by the Saviour, about a private hotline to God in prayer. That is all very well, provided

the relationship with Jesus energises one to show Christ's concern for the poor and sick, and for the values which underpin our society. As one writer, John Robinson, put it, 'The test of worship is how far it makes us more sensitive to the beyond in our midst, to the Christ in the hungry, the naked, the homeless and the prisoners.'

Some years ago, at a Eucharistic Congress, the Archbishop of Khartoum in Sudan raised a challenging question: 'If we break bread in the sanctuary but do not break it outside the sanctuary while there are a thousand people in my diocese dying from hunger each day, how can we say that our Eucharist is valid?' Questions about the Eucharist usually refer to what is happening to the bread and wine on the altar. But in the early Christian centuries, the questions were more about what is happening to the community who are celebrating. One great preacher from the period, St John Chrysotom, John of the Golden Mouth, has left us a very challenging sermon about honouring the Lord. In it he says the following:

> Would you honour the body of Christ? Do not despise him in his nakedness; do not honour him here in church clothed in silk vestments and then pass him by unclothed and frozen outside.
>
> God has no need of golden vessels but of golden hearts.
>
> Make your house beautiful by all means but also look after the poor, or rather look after the poor first. No one has ever condemned for not

adorning his house, but those who neglect the poor are threatened with hellfire for all eternity.

'Give them something to eat yourselves.'
Jesus gave a glimpse of his power in providing for people's hunger that day when he multiplied the loaves and fishes. This miracle anticipated the changing of bread and wine into his living presence as the food of our pilgrimage of life. On the day that he fed the multitude he engaged the apostles in organising the crowd, in distributing the food and in gathering the leftovers. This engagement in action anticipates the mission given to all who receive the Lord in the Bread of Life. We have a saying that there is no such thing as a free meal. The Eucharist is a wonderful gift of God's love. But with the gift comes the responsibility of passing on the message and reality of Christ's love to others. We are to move from Mass into mission when we are solemnly dismissed to go in peace and to love and serve the Lord.

To the words of dismissal we respond: 'Thanks be to God.'
Not in the weary sense of relief that the ceremony is over. No, we are thanking God who has fed us on his word and in the Eucharist: and thanking God for honouring us with a mission of bringing his love out of the church to wherever people are hungry or in a lonely place.

'Lord the people are hungry and this is a lonely place.' What he tells us is to give them something to eat ourselves. Christ is counting on you.

# EUCHARIST
# AND JUSTICE

SIXTH SUNDAY IN ORDINARY TIME: YEAR A

# THE EUCHARIST AND JUSTICE

*Dermot Lane, Balally, Dublin*

*'So when you are offering your gift at the altar, if you remember that your brother or sister has something against you...' (Matthew 5:23).* This familiar sentence from the Sermon on the Mount leaves us in no doubt about the action we must take. The connection between Eucharist and the work of justice and reconciliation is clear. This sentence is part of the Gospel reading from St Matthew's Sermon on the Mount read on 6th Sunday in Ordinary Time, Year A. It is also read on Friday, First Week of Lent and Thursday, 10th Week in Ordinary Time. It is given as a reading on the occasion of the dedication of an altar.

This Gospel reading contains part two of Matthew's Sermon on the Mount which deals with some key sayings of Jesus (17-20) and a series of antitheses or contrast statements (21-37/48).

The sayings of Jesus make it quite explicit that he did not come to abolish the law but instead to fulfil it and this is a theme that runs throughout Matthew's Gospel. Judaism is the matrix of Christianity. For Matthew, Jesus is the flowering of the hope of Israel and not therefore the abolition or the abrogation or the replacement of Judaism. For too long, Christianity saw itself as superseding Judaism, that is, putting an end to Judaism or, even worse, replacing it. This self-understanding of Christianity has had tragic consequences for Jews in history and is one of key factors that facilitated the horror of Holocaust in Nazi Germany.

The Second Vatican Council put an end to this distorted understanding of Christianity by pointing out that the Jews still remain most dear to God, that God does not repent of the gifts he makes nor of the call he issues (*Nostra Aetate*, 4). This point cannot be made too often in contemporary preaching and we need to remember how Pope John Paul II went to the Western Wall in Jerusalem in the Jubilee Year 2000 to pray for forgiveness of sins against Jews.

A series of contrast statements comes after the sayings of Jesus and each contrast is introduced with the expression: 'You have heard that it was said ... but I say to you...' Each statement contains a contrast between the traditional understanding of the law and the teaching of Jesus.

Within this homily, I want to focus on the contrast statement made by Jesus in relation to worship: 'So when you are offering your gift at the altar, if you remember that your brother or sister has something against you, leave your gift there before the altar and go; first be reconciled to your brother or sister, and then come and offer your gift' (v. 23).

There are a number of important issues contained in this statement by Jesus. First of all, it presupposes worship in the temple and that at this stage in his ministry Jesus respected this worship in the temple while at the same time strongly disapproving of those who worship without attending to right relationships.

In effect, Jesus is saying there can be no authentic worship of God without prior attention to the healing of personal relationships. A fundamental link exists between the celebration of the Eucharist and the work of justice. Jesus gives priority to ethics over cult.

In this regard, Jesus is recovering the teachings of the prophets in the Hebrew Scriptures. Many of the prophets before him, such as Amos, Isaiah and Jeremiah, were outspoken in their condemnation of worship that neglected the work of justice. Listen to the words of Amos:

> The Lord says,
> 'I hate your religious festivals.
> I cannot stand them.
> When you bring your burnt offerings
> And green offerings
> I will not accept them.
> Stop your noisy songs,
> I do not want to listen to your harps.
> Instead let justice flow like a stream
> And righteousness like a river that never
> goes dry'. (Amos 5/ 21-25)

This link between worship and justice is taken up again later on in the ministry of Jesus: 'Go and learn what this means. "I desire mercy, and not sacrifice"' (Matthew 9:3; cf. Hosea 6:6).

And then, towards the end of his life, as if to drive home this teaching, Jesus links the institution of the Eucharist at the

Last Supper with the prophetic action of washing the feet of his disciples.

This teaching of the prophets and especially of Jesus is as important today as it was two thousand years ago. It is a teaching that should disturb all of us who dare to celebrate the Eucharist. It is also a teaching that young people often level against Mass-goers: look at x who goes to Mass, but rides roughshod over his or her relationships with others, especially in matters of justice.

As a worshipping community, we must attend to the link between the celebration of the Eucharist and the work of justice, between the adoration of Christ in the Eucharist and the importance of caring for others, between the comforting presence of Christ in the Eucharist and the disturbing presence of Christ in the poor.

Those who celebrate the Eucharist cannot therefore be indifferent to the plight of the poor in society. Every celebration of the Eucharist concludes with the challenging statement: 'Go in peace to love and serve the Lord', that is, go out into the world to put into practice the communion 'in Christ' that we have celebrated, especially in regard to those who are in need. If we fail to recognise Christ in the poor and the hungry and the marginalised, then there is something essential missing in the celebration of the Eucharist.

In 1981, the international Eucharistic Congress at Lourdes took for its theme: 'Bread broken for a New World'. This particular theme sought to bring out the essential connection between the celebration of the Eucharist and the responsibility upon all Christians to build a better and more just world. Of course, perfect justice can never be realised in this life until the Kingdom of God arrives at the end of time, but in the meantime we are all called to sow the seeds of the Kingdom of God in and through the work of justice.

In 2004, John Paul II returned to this theme in his apostolic letter, *Mane nobiscum Domine*. In that document he points out that the celebration of 'the Eucharist gives to the community ... a practical commitment to building a more just and fraternal society'. This practical commitment to justice, said John Paul II, 'affects the authenticity of the communal sharing in the Eucharist' (28). Without this commitment to the work of justice an essential element is missing in our celebration of the Eucharist. This is the teaching of the prophets of Israel, the explicit teaching of Jesus of Nazareth, and the teaching of John Paul II.

Is it possible that our celebration of the Eucharist could become a source of action for justice in the world? Each celebration of the Eucharist has the capacity to send us out to work for justice and to feed the hunger of the world. And likewise: is it possible that the struggle for justice and equality might begin to impact on the way we celebrate the Eucharist?

To sum up: there are ethical presuppositions that should inform our celebration of the Eucharist and equally important there are ethical consequences that flow from the celebration of the Eucharist.

# Holy Thursday

## Like Jesus who Serves

*Martin Hogan PC, Drumcondra, Dublin*

*The Lord's gift of himself is a privileged way in which the Lord continues to serve us. In return we must become the servants that he is calling us to be. The service that marks Holy Thursday is often expressed in the liturgy through the involvement of those active in community and parish life and those who act as ministers in liturgy. Such service, of course, is not confined to this one special evening.*

Holy Thursday is all about service. When Jesus washed the feet of his disciples, he was serving them in a very simple but very loving way. The service that Jesus performed for them on Holy Thursday was only a sign of a much greater service that he would perform for the disciples and for all of us on the following day. On Thursday he laid down his garments to wash his disciples' feet. On Friday he would lay down his life for them and for all of us gathered here today. Jesus spoke of himself as the one who came not to be served but to serve and to give his life for many.

# Like Jesus who Serves

Our calling as followers of Jesus is to love one another as he has loved us, to serve one another as he has served us. We are called to be Holy Thursday people, people who stand ready to serve one another. Parents who have brought their children here to this Mass are Holy Thursday people, because they serve their children every day. In a sense, children make servants of us all, but in particular of their parents! Parents care for their children in a whole variety of ways every day, seeing to it that they are washed and clothed and fed and provided for. This is the service that Holy Thursday celebrates and honours. When children become adults they often find themselves caring in various ways for their parents. Our parents who spend so long caring for us often come to need our care when they become old and infirm. The care that adult men and women give to their parents is another expression of the service that Holy Thursday celebrates and honours. The family is the basic context in which we live out the Lord's call in today's Gospel reading to wash each other's feet, to serve one another as he has served us.

There are all kinds of other services that people render outside the context of their families. We might think of those who provide opportunities for children to be engaged in various sporting activities. So often, the running of football clubs and other sports clubs is dependant on people who are prepared to give their time and energy to train youngsters, to referee matches, to organise competitions and so on. Service, in the strict sense, is work done on behalf of others without looking for any financial reward. Thankfully there are many people in our communities who are still willing to serve in that sense.

We might think this Holy Thursday of all those people who serve in a variety of ways in the local parish community. The family Mass group who put time and energy into children's liturgies in the parish are true servants in that Gospel sense. This Holy Thursday is a very appropriate day on which to thank them for their generous service to the children of the parish. Many people serve the parish community in a great many other ways. There are those who ensure that the older people of our community are given opportunities to live life to the full, and to continue to develop their gifts and talents. Many other parishioners offer their services as readers, as Eucharistic ministers, as collectors, as members of the choir, the baptism team, the liturgy group, the communications group, the parish pastoral council and so on. We sometimes take our servants for granted because they are always there, just as when we were children we often took our parents for granted. Holy Thursday is a good day on which to remember our servants, to give thanks to God for them, to express our appreciation to them and to encourage them.

In today's Gospel reading, Peter resisted the service that Jesus wanted to perform for him. Peter said to Jesus, 'Never! You shall never wash my feet'. He tried to prevent Jesus from serving him. Sometimes we too can block people from serving us. Perhaps we feel that we can manage best on our own, that we do not need the service that someone is offering us. Yet, in reality, whereas we all have something to give to others, we all have something to receive from others as well. We all need each other's gifts and services. As St Paul says in one of his letters, 'The eye cannot say to the hand, "I have no need of you", nor can the head say to the feet, "I have no need of you".' We are called both to serve others and to receive the service of others. On this Holy Thursday we pray not only for the willingness to serve but also for the openness to receive the service that the Lord wants to offer us through the members of his body.

Very shortly we will be invited to the altar to receive the Lord in the Eucharist. The Lord, who washed the feet of his disciples at the last supper, also gave them the gift of himself under the form of bread and wine. The Lord continues to give us that same gift of himself in the Eucharist this evening. The Lord's gift of himself in the Eucharist is a privileged way in which the Lord continues to serve us today. We need this particular service that the Lord offers us through the Eucharist if we are to become the servants that he is calling us all to be.

## Twentieth Sunday in Ordinary Time: Year B

# Strength to Serve

*John Watts PP, Holy Innocents Church, Southwark*

*Knowing that the hour had come, Jesus gathers his disciples together. St John begins his account of the lengthy discourse of that evening with the washing of the feet, a profound example of service. Jesus, the Bread of Life, gives us the Eucharistic food to strengthen us to serve one another. The Gospel of Holy Thursday's Evening Mass of the Lord's Supper is the account of the washing of the feet. On 29th Sunday in Ordinary Time, Year B we hear in the Gospel (John 6:51-58) that Jesus is the living bread. 'Anyone who eats this bread will live for ever.'*

It often seems strange that in the Gospel of St John, we find no record of the institution of the Eucharist. This is left to the synoptic Gospels. When we reach the account of the last supper in St John's Gospel, we find the simple but profound action of Jesus washing the disciples' feet, an act that they found hard to understand. Perhaps two thousand years later we are no different.

To find the Lord's teaching on the Eucharist in the Gospel of St John, we turn back the pages from the Last Supper to a desert scene and the feeding of a vast crowd. But St John is a clever writer with his insertion that these events took place 'shortly before the Jewish Feast of Passover'. He wants to take us back to the Upper Room. Perhaps it is timely that during this Summer season, several months after the Sacred Triduum, the Lectionary focuses our attention on the teaching of the Lord about the gift of Himself in the Eucharist.

In today's section the focus is upon the food and drink that the Lord offers – 'for my flesh is real drink and my blood is real drink.' If we are to have like then this is the food and drink that we need. Our daily need for food and drink is obvious, without them we die; there is only a limited period that we can survive without nourishment. Ours is an age of healthy eating; we are given constant reminders of the need for a balanced diet. Books regularly appear telling us 'we are what we eat'.

Isn't Jesus speaking today about a balanced diet, the food and drink we need to be his faithful followers and servants. 'If you do not eat the flesh of the Son of Man and drink his blood you will not have life in you'. What does it mean to eat the body of the Lord and drink his blood if not to become more like him? It was Pope Leo the Great who coined the phrase that when we receive the body of the Lord, we become the body of Christ:

> For our participation in the body and blood of Christ has this effect: it makes us become what we receive; it enables us, with our whole being, in our spirit and our flesh, to bear him in whom and

with whom we have died and been buried and risen again.

(Sermon 12 on The Passion)

By being one with the Lord in the Eucharist we make present the saving events of the passion, death and resurrection as Pope John Paul II reminded in the encyclical *Ecclesia de Eucharistia*. We are taken back to the Upper Room:

> At every celebration of the Eucharist, we are spiritually brought back to the Paschal Triduum: to the events of Holy Thursday, to the Last Supper and to what followed it. (3)

As we contemplate the scene in the Upper Room we not only see Jesus gathered with the twelve, we also hear the words, 'Do this in memory of me' and we witness the act of love and service which Jesus performs as he washes the feet of his disciples. Eucharist and service, interwoven and inseparable! It is the living out of the truth 'that he came not to be served but to serve' and that this will be the hallmark of the followers of this Servant.

So we come to realise the connection between the gift of the Eucharist and the washing of the feet. This connection was acknowledged in the late Pope's Letter for the Year of the Eucharist, *Mane nobiscum Domine*:

> It is not by chance that the Gospel of John contains no account of the institution of the Eucharist, but instead relates the washing of feet (cf. John 13:1-20): by bending down to wash the

feet of his disciples, Jesus explains the meaning of the Eucharist unequivocally (28).

'Love one another' will take many forms. It can be the simple act of giving a listening ear or speaking the affirming word to a distressed friend. Maybe it is a life of committed service and love to the care of a sick patient. It is through the Eucharist when the Lord gives us his life that we can start to be his followers and servants and give that life to others.

Sixth Sunday in Ordinary Time: Year C

# Blessed are You Who Are Poor

*Dermot Lane PP, Balally, Dublin*

*The Beatitudes are a prophetic reminder that wealth can become an obstacle between God and us. The Eucharist calls us to liberation and inclusion so that, as St Paul teaches, we may form a single body, sharing in the one Bread. Luke's Sermon on the Plain (6:17.20-26) with its four Beatitudes and four 'woes.' is read on 6th Sunday in Ordinary Time and, as we end the year, on Wednesday, 33rd Week in Ordinary Time. The Pauline references are read: 1 Cor 10:16-17 on the feast of Corpus Christi, Year A and 1 Cor 11:20-22 on Monday, 24th Week in Ordinary Time, Year II.*

Our Gospel reading gives us what is known as Luke's Sermon on the Plain, which is a shorter and probably earlier version of Matthew's Sermon on the Mount.

Luke's Sermon is made up of four beatitudes and each beatitude has a corresponding 'woe'. The purpose of the four 'woes' is to help us understand in a balanced way the full meaning of the beatitudes.

# Blessed Are You Who Are Poor

The Sermon on the Plain only makes sense in the context of the preaching and practice of Jesus concerning the coming reign of God. The reign of God proclaimed by Jesus is about the establishment of right relations between rich and poor, men and women, humanity and God.

'Blessed are you who are poor, for yours is the Kingdom of God'. Why should the poor be blessed? Because the poor in Luke know better than most about their need of salvation and therefore appreciate the importance of the coming reign of God.

Then comes the 'woe'. 'Woe to you who are rich, for you have received your consolation'. By contrast, the rich are content with their present lot in life and therefore have no need of Jesus and the coming reign of God.

The kingdom of God proclaimed by Jesus demands something of a revolution in the life of the individual, a radical personal conversion, a turning upside-down of things in one's life. It is within this new situation that the poor are rich and the hungry will be fulfilled and those who mourn will laugh.

The inevitable and obvious question arises here: Does this mean that to enter the kingdom of God one must become materially poor? No, but it does mean that money must not become an end in itself. As an end in itself, money becomes an idol and distracts us from God and the need to acknowledge our dependence on God. Ultimately only God – and not mammon – can save us.

How are we to make sense of these beatitudes of Luke in a world in which economic success is the criterion of everything and material well-being is a status symbol? The Beatitudes are a prophetic reminder to all that being rich can become a barrier between the individual and God, between being a disciple of Jesus and membership of the reign of God.

On more than one occasion, Jesus warns against riches. He points out: 'Truly I tell you, it will be hard for a rich person to enter the kingdom of God. Again I tell you it is easier for a camel to go through the eye of a needle than for someone who is rich to enter the kingdom of God' (Matthew 19: 23-24; Mark 10: 23-25).

It is important to note that the teaching of Jesus on poverty is multi-layered. As such, Jesus is not holding up material poverty as a norm for discipleship, though it can be a norm for a small number of monastic or religious individuals who wish to point towards the reign of God in this world. Instead, Jesus recognises that it is the poor who know their need for salvation and therefore find it easier to appreciate the importance of the coming reign of God.

It is important to point out, also, that there is nothing beautiful about being poor. To the contrary, Jesus goes out of his way to alleviate poverty, not by alms-giving, but by empowering the poor through the introduction of a new kind of table to fellowship which he formalises towards the end of his life at the Last Supper.

In the light of this approach by Jesus to the poor, we have to ask ourselves how and to what extent does the celebration of the Eucharist today empower participants to become agents of liberation and social justice in our world. For example, John Chrysostom establishes an important link between the celebration of the Eucharist and the work of justice, between commitment to Christ in the Eucharist and commitment to Christ in the poor. He points out:

> Do you wish to honour the body of Christ?
> Do not despise him when he is naked.

> Do not honour him here in the church building with silks, only to neglect him outside, when he is suffering from cold and nakedness.
>
> For he who said: 'this is my Body', is the same who said: 'you saw me, a hungry man, and you did not give me to eat'...
>
> Feed the hungry and then come and decorate the table'.

It is quite clear, therefore, that the Sermon on the Plain is explicitly counter-cultural, that is it contains a critique of the culture at the time of Jesus and of our contemporary culture today.

The strongest sacramental expression of this counter-cultural character of the preaching of Jesus is to be found in the celebration of the Eucharist. The Eucharist ought to be a place where the poor and mourners, the hungry and the despised, are made to feel welcome and experience hospitality. The liberating power of the Eucharist should be experienced by all within the celebration of the Eucharist.

Equally, the celebration of the Eucharist should be that place where the rich, the well-fed, those who laugh and the well-spoken should experience the full weight of the woes of Jesus. In other words, the prophetic role of the Eucharist should be apparent for those who are well-off. In this way, the Eucharist should comfort the disturbed and, at the same time, disturb the comfortable.

Every celebration of the Eucharist should seek to overcome the social divide that exists between the rich and the poor, between the well-fed and the hungry and in this way bring about a new unity between the rich and the poor within the one Body of Christ.

In St Paul's theology of the celebration of the Eucharist, he seeks to overcome this particular divide between rich and poor. Paul points out:

> The fact that there is only one loaf means that though there are many of us, we form a single body because we all share in this one loaf.
> (1 Corinthians 10:16-17)

If this transformation and unity that the Eucharist seeks to bring about does not happen, then there is something missing within the celebration of the Eucharist. This was, in fact, a problem for the early Christians at the church in Corinth, where the celebration of the Eucharist was closely connected with the celebration of communal meals. Within that context, Paul condemns the celebration of the Eucharist alongside these communal meals which allow the old social divisions and separations to exist. Paul speaks out strongly against this inconsistency between the celebration of the Eucharist and the sharing of communal meals:

> It is not the Lord's Supper that you are eating, since when the time comes to eat, everyone is in such a hurry to start his own supper that one person goes hungry while another is getting drunk.
> (1 Corinthians 11: 20-22)

In effect, Paul is complaining against the inconsistency between the celebration of unity within the Eucharist alongside the existence of social separations and divisions within the communal meals at Corinth. If the equality and unity and solidarity that belongs to the celebration of the Eucharist are missing within the communal meals, then there is something wrong with the way the Eucharist is celebrated.

# EUCHARIST AND MISSION

## Tenth Sunday in Ordinary Time: Year B

# Receiving Eternal Life

*Aidan Troy CP, Holy Cross, Ardoyne, Belfast.*

*In a world of conflict and change, the disciple of Christ lives in confident waiting. But in receiving Christ in the Eucharist we know that we do not have to wait until the next life to receive eternal life. We already possess it! The Gospel reading, Mark 3:20-35, and the Genesis story of the Fall, read on 10th Sunday in Ordinary Time, Year B help us to place this faith in reality.*

I find it rather difficult not to judge. Despite my best efforts I am often assessing the person rather than what they are saying or what they are doing. I know it is wrong and I lose so much of the richness that someone has for me.

When Jesus started out to reveal the Kingdom, judgement came hot and heavy. His own relatives 'set out to take charge of him, convinced he was out of his mind.' (Mark 3:21)

The scribes who had come down from Jerusalem and who should have known better, weighed in with 'Beelzebul is in him' and 'It is through the prince of devils that he casts out devils.' (Mark 3:22)

Even the Mother of Jesus and brothers arrive asking for him. Were they also worried about him? Did they judge that he needs to come home as it was becoming too dangerous?

From the dawn of creation the struggle between God and Satan, good and evil, has been waged. The nakedness of Adam in the garden created fear when he heard the voice of God. The man knew he was wrong and sought at once to offload the blame. So, 'it was the woman you put with me, she gave me the fruit and I ate it.' (Genesis 3:12) The woman in turn put the blame on the serpent. Each is judging and blaming the other for what was fundamentally his or her own sin. How often I will point anywhere to avoid accepting what is my responsibility. It is so much easier to 'explain' what happened in terms of what someone else did. But at some deeper level when I am forced to face my inner demons I know the truth and if accepted I can be free.

The Genesis story can never be told (or read) often enough. In the first creation story of Genesis we find not some ideal age long lost, but a glimpse of what God did and does: male and female God created in the image of God and equal (Genesis 1:27). In the second Creation story of Genesis we are reminded of the two as one body, one flesh (Genesis 2:24). Yet almost from the beginning, darker forces are also there and at work. There is disobedience and arrogance. By their actions we see the man and woman disturb the harmony of paradise, alienating them from the God who created them. By their actions they establish an ambiguous relationship between themselves and the rest of creation.

Into this world Jesus enters and comes as the second Adam. He will not conform to what some people had expected and thought as fitting and right. God being made in the image of a human's preference is not new. People have always tried to manage God in a way that they see fit. But to do this boundaries and limitations have to be set. Jesus came as the great boundary breaker and the revelation of God.

I am good at drawing lines, real or symbolic, between people. I am good at making moral judgements about people. When I do these things I reverse the seamlessness of God's creation. My act of division leads to dominance and destruction, inclusion and exclusion, hierarchy and privilege. My actions lead to 'us' and 'them'. In a Northern context there is the cancer of sectarianism. It runs so deep that if you scratch the surface there it is racing through my veins. I keep it so well disguised and speak so liberally that I can deceive myself as I mislead others.

There was a time in Ireland when people from other countries were few and far between. Now my neighbours show forth the beauty and variety of God's creation. It sounds lovely and in my better moments I would want to welcome them all. But racism is not the preserve of right-wing groups. It is alive and well in suburbs and villages, in cities and towns.

In this liturgy Jesus is establishing priorities. In the new dispensation to be a disciple is paramount. Yes, to be a disciple is more fundamental than kinship. The heart of being a disciple is to be receptive in all sorts of ways: receptiveness to God's word, receptiveness to God's will: 'Anyone who does the will of God, that person is my brother and sister and mother.' (Mark 3:35)

Some well-meaning people are surprised, even shocked, at the scene when the Mother of Jesus arrived and 'sent in a message asking for him.' (Mark 3:31) But look at Mary as the Second Eve. She was never disobedient, but from conception to cross is at one with God's will. She is a member of both families – blood and discipleship. Mary did not need to shift the blame as happened in the Garden. Obedience to the will of God is Mary's great strength. Mary stood on Calvary and watched and waited. She was helpless to do anything. Any image of her as serene and coping well may miss the inner struggle of Mary. I believe that Simeon's sword of sorrow came back to her at this moment. Now she knows that putting her hand into God's hand has a cost. She doesn't turn and walk away. I wish I could say the same in my own life.

The Eucharist has not changed. But so much around the Eucharist today bears signs of cross and often gives a negative impression. There is a decline in vocations to priesthood in so many countries. Parish after parish is reducing the number of celebrations of the Eucharist at weekends. Parishes are being described as being 'clustered' or some such phrase. The number assembling for Mass in many parishes is declining. It would be easy to become downhearted and sad. Maybe amidst all this suffering we need to see the resurrection dimension. 'The acclamation of the assembly following the consecration appropriately ends by expressing the eschatological thrust which marks the celebration of the Eucharist (cf. 1 Corinthians 11:26): 'until you come in glory' ... In the Eucharist everything speaks of confident waiting ... Those who feed on Christ in the Eucharist need not wait until the hereafter to receive eternal life: they already possess it on earth, as the first fruits of a future fullness which will embrace people in their totality' (John Paul II: *Ecclesia de Eucharista*, 18)

Whatever is happening in and around us we have to remain resolute:

## Receving Eternal Life

I will walk in the presence of the Lord, in the land of the living.

*Psalm 114:9*

## Body and Blood of Christ (Corpus Christi): Year C

# From East to West

### Martin Hogan PC, Drumcondra, Dublin

*The Body and Blood of Christ is the gift that broadens our horizons so that we may enter the Lord's generous vision. This homily was prepared for the solemnity of the Body and Blood of Christ (Corpus Christi), Year C.*

The Latin term 'Corpus Christi' may not be easily understood by many people today. The title, 'The Body and Blood of Christ' is probably more intelligible. Today is the feast of the Eucharist, a day when we give thanks for the gift of the Eucharist, through which the Lord is present among us in a very special way.

In the opening pages of his encyclical on the Eucharist, Pope John Paul II recalls the many places in which he has celebrated the Eucharist. He mentions that he celebrated Mass in the great basilicas and churches in Rome and throughout the world, in chapels built along mountain paths, on lakeshores and seacoasts, on altars built in stadiums and in city squares. He remarks that the great variety of places where he has celebrated Mass has given him a powerful experience of the universal and cosmic character of the Eucharist. As he puts it, 'even when the Eucharist is celebrated on the humble altar of a country church, it is always in some way celebrated on the altar of the world'. The Eucharist, he says, 'embraces and permeates all creation'.

In John's Gospel, Jesus, speaking of his death, says: 'When I am lifted up from the earth, I will draw all people to myself'. He gave his life in love so as to draw all people to himself and to the God who sent him. It is that self-giving love of Jesus unto death that we celebrate in the Eucharist and that is present to us there. Christ present in the Eucharist continues to draw all people, all of creation, to himself. That is why, whenever we gather to celebrate the Eucharist, we are invited to think globally, to remember all of humanity, all of creation. Many of the prayers of the Mass reflect that universal character of the Eucharist. At the beginning of the third Eucharistic prayer, we pray: 'Father... from age to age you gather a people to yourself, so that from east to west a perfect offering may be made to the glory of your name'. In the fourth Eucharistic prayer, we pray, 'Source of life and goodness, you have created all things to fill your creatures with every blessing and lead all people to the joyful vision of your light'.

The Eucharist will always invite us to broaden our horizons, to look beyond ourselves, beyond our families, beyond our parish, beyond our Diocese, beyond the church, towards all of humanity and all of creation. The Eucharist puts it up to us to have the same breath of vision that Jesus had. Something of that breath of vision of Jesus is reflected in today's Gospel reading. The crowds to whom Jesus had been ministering had grown hungry. The disciples suggested that Jesus send the crowds away. Their suggestion revealed a certain narrowness of vision on their part. They wanted the problem crowd removed from the scene. However, Jesus' horizon was wider than that of his disciples. He could not forget the hungry crowd so easily. He challenged his disciples to engage with the crowd. 'Give them something to eat yourselves', he said to them. The disciples resisted Jesus' suggestion, claiming that the task was beyond them, 'We have no more than five loaves and two fish'. Jesus went on to show them that he could work powerfully with their limited resources and that, with his help, the task they had considered impossible was indeed manageable. Jesus enabled his disciples to feed the very crowd they had been so keen to dismiss.

We might be able to recognise something of ourselves in the disciples. We too can be tempted to send people away, to keep our distance from those we suspect might make demands on us. We can allow our horizons to become narrowed to what we consider to be manageable. The Lord in the Eucharist will always prompt us to look beyond our own narrow circle and to enter more fully into his own generous vision. In the second reading this morning Paul tells us that Jesus instituted the Eucharist 'on the night he was betrayed'. Those words of Paul bring us back to the dramatic setting in which the Eucharist was born. The Eucharist is intimately linked to the events of the Lord's passion and death. The Lord's death on the cross was a death for all, an expression of a love that knows no measure. It is that love for all unto the end that is present to us every time we celebrate the Eucharist. The late Pope John Paul II, in his encyclical letter on the Eucharist, refers to the 'universal charity of the Eucharistic sacrifice'.

Whenever we celebrate the Eucharist, we are expressing our desire that something of this universal charity of Christ we are celebrating would be present in our own lives. To celebrate the Eucharist is to commit ourselves to the same generous vision that characterised Jesus' life and death, the vision whose instinct it is to feed the hungry crowd rather than send them away. The invitation we are given at Mass to offer each other the sign of peace is a small reminder of the call the Eucharist makes on us to move beyond our own narrow circle. As Christ challenged his disciples in today's Gospel reading, the Eucharist challenges us to engage with, to serve, people we might initially be tempted to send away. Today on the feast of Corpus Christi we give thanks for the many people in our parish and beyond who live the Eucharist they celebrate, who make present in their own lives something of the universal charity of Christ. We pray that our own vision and concern would in some way be stretched by the universal sacrifice of the Eucharist that we celebrate every Sunday.

# Eighteenth Sunday in Ordinary Time: Year C

## The Table of Inclusion

*Frank Murray PP, Ferbane, Co. Offaly*

*To a world of greed, Jesus preaches a message of caring for one another and of fellowship. The Eucharist is a table of fellowship and inclusion. The parable of the rich man is read on 18th Sunday in Ordinary Time, Year C and also on Monday, Week 29. The teaching on storing up true treasure is also repeated in Matthew 6:19-21, which is the Gospel of 8th Sunday in Ordinary Time, Year A.*

I will pull down my barns and build bigger ones, and store all my grain and goods in them. And I will say to my soul... eat, drink and have a good time...

The Eucharist is the table of inclusion. Jesus is God's bread from heaven to feed the world. Jesus is the Holy Eucharist of God to feed the family of humanity. Jesus is the table of friendship where nobody grows old. Jesus in the sheer simplicity and poverty of the Eucharist, always linked to the washed feet, pulls down the barns of wealth and greed.

# The Table of Inclusion

Jesus is forever the critique of that which is given to us as gift and which we accumulate for ourselves to the exclusion of others.

> I was hungry and you gave me food.
> I was thirsty and you gave me to drink.

On this alone will we be judged. Did we share the Bread of Life, or did we build bigger and think smaller?

There is a modern parable about a man who died and went to heaven. There at the gate of heaven he was met by the Lord who made him welcome. The man asked a favour of the Lord. He asked could he go down and take a peep at hell before he entered his heavenly home? The Lord smilingly agreed and led him down a winding staircase to the gates of hell. When the door was opened he was amazed. He saw, not a blazing furnace, but a beautiful banquet room lit by magnificent chandeliers and furnished with exquisite taste. In the centre was a great table, covered with fine linen and containing the most wonderful food, beautifully laid out and delicious to the eye and nostrils. Around the table sat all the people in fine dress. On closer inspection the man noticed that there was something wrong. All the people were affected by a strange malaise. They could not bend their elbows. The food was there but try as they might they could not get the food into their mouths. They were all dying of hunger in the midst of plenty.

This, the man noted, was hell and so he asked the Lord to take him back to the heavenly place. The Lord led him to the door of Paradise. When the door opened what did the man see, only the room of hell exactly replicated in every detail, lights, furnishings and the great table in the centre, laid with food 'to

## At the Breaking of Bread

take the sight out of your eye'. Here in heaven the people will be able to bend their elbows, the man thought with satisfaction. But no... exactly as it was in hell; the people were affected by the same paralysis of the elbow! But wait... the man noticed a great difference... here in heaven nobody was hungry. Here the people feed each other. Everyone looked after the other. Hell and heaven are the same place. The people make the difference.

The logic of our consumer world, based on the principle of success and competition is to build bigger barns, for bigger profits. It is the logic of our consumer world that more is better. Power is success. Profit is prize and accumulation is all. It is the Gospel of greed. It is the place of hell.

The logic of the Holy Eucharist goes against the grain. It is the Gospel of gift and graciousness. Small is beautiful; the Sermon on the Mount is simplicity. The Eucharist, the Bread of Life taken, blessed, broken and shared... is always shared, for the life of the world, the starving world. Our Eucharist has its roots in the Passover Meal of the Jewish people.

This is a prayer prayed at the Passover meal...

> Among people everywhere the sharing of bread forms a band of fellowship. For the sake of our redemption we say together the ancient words which join us with our own people, and with all people who are in need, with the wrongly imprisoned and the beggar in the street. For our redemption is tied up with the deliverance from bondage of people everywhere.

In his letter for us for the Year of the Eucharist, Pope John Paul II, a Pope who knew suffering, wrote:

# The Table of Inclusion

The Eucharist is a project of solidarity for all humanity... The Christian who takes part in the Eucharist learns to become the promoter of communion, peace and solidarity in every situation... In the Eucharist our God has shown Love in the extreme overturning all the criteria of power which often governs human relations and radically affirming the criterion of service (Mark 9:35)... Our troubled world demands that Christians learn to experience the Eucharist as a great school of peace, forming men and women who can become promoters of dialogue and communion...

It is not only by chance that the Gospel of John contains no account of the Institution of the Eucharist but instead relates the 'washing of the feet' (John 13:1-20). By bending down to wash the feet of the disciples, Jesus explains the meaning of the Eucharist unequivocally...

*Mane nobiscum Domine*

Seventeenth Sunday in Ordinary Time: Year B

# Communion and Ecumenism

*Ken O'Riordan,*
*Adult Education Adviser for the Diocese of Nottingham*

*The feeding of the crowd is told in the four Gospels. Matthew, Mark and Luke begin by Jesus suggesting sending away the crowd but John has Jesus asking Philip, 'Where can we buy some bread for these people to eat?' We live in pain in a world that is able to share with those in need. As Christians there is also the pain of division; we are not able to share the Eucharist. Throughout the year and especially during the annual Week of Prayer for Christian Unity we pray 'that all may be one.' St John's account of the feeding of the crowd (6:1-15) is read on 17th Sunday in Ordinary Time, Year B. It is also read on Friday, 2nd week of Easter.*

A friend of mine, the Reverend Mary Stevens, who was one of the first women to be ordained into the Anglican Priesthood at Lincoln Cathedral, invited me to preach at her first celebration of the Eucharist in her parish of St Martin's in Grimsby. I was delighted to accept the invitation and I preached about the importance of Communion between the Churches.

When we came to the communion rite of the celebration, I along with the fairly large Catholic community present, went forward to receive a blessing from Mary. I was particularly struck by the presence of a retired senior priest, who was sharing the presbytery with me, literally struggling forward to receive a blessing. Mary Stevens was deeply moved and felt greatly supported by the Catholic Community that night, although the pain of us not being able to share fully in communion was also strikingly present.

In the following weeks between twenty or thirty parishioners made it their business to speak to me. The gist of what they said was, 'It was really good to be there and, you know, for the first time I felt the pain of not being able to receive communion.' My own reflection was: 'Wouldn't it be great if we endlessly felt the pain of those who, for whatever reason, can't receive communion with us. And felt that pain not just for the members of our own families who no longer go to church or for those within our community who are unable to receive communion, but also for those of other Christian denominations outside our community.'

The question put by Jesus to Philip in the Gospel story, 'Where can we buy (or perhaps get) some bread for these people to eat?', offers both an opportunity and a challenge.

That question, if we kept repeating it, not just within Church circles but also in the political arena would surely demand an answer. The pain of not being able to share our bread with those in need would take on a life of its own and seek expression in a profound solidarity particularly with the poor of our world. The apparently simple action at the heart of the Gospel story of Jesus taking the loaves, giving thanks and giving out as much as was wanted lies at the heart of every Eucharist and is a constant thorn in the side to all who would receive communion.

To receive communion is to be in union with Jesus, but it is also to be in union with all who receive and with all in need of the bread of life. There is something radically wrong with simply feeding oneself while others go hungry. This mystery of solidarity is of the essence of what it is to be in communion, whether it is possible to receive the sacrament or not at this present time.

It is a truth, which challenges us personally, nationally and internationally and will not go away. Our own history has been that of economic migrants, of refugees of living from hand to mouth, working at hard and difficult jobs, sending money home to keep families alive. Surely we shouldn't forget now that we are economically so much better off! The mystery of sharing in the Gospel story, the discovery that there is enough and that if we share there will always be plenty left over offers a critique of much which tends to be promoted today.

The pain experienced by so many at the celebration at St Martin's in Grimsby was surely a profound expression of true ecumenism and of true human solidarity. A recognition of brokenness, without bitterness, a commitment to work together and celebrate difference – an understanding of the deeper communion which will one day find expression in the sharing of the breaking of bread.

MISSION SUNDAY

# MISSION

### Gerry French SSC

*Every Christian is called to be a missionary. This is our baptismal calling that is constantly renewed in Eucharist. Mission Sunday is observed on the second last Sunday of October each year. Our best way of keeping this day is our gathering to hear God's word and to celebrate Eucharist.*

Some years ago I was showing a Mission film in a hall in Birmingham on the old style projector – Bill, a Co. Offaly man, was helping me with the intemperate machine – he heard me respond to questions about the missionary life and the missionary vocations. As we put the reel back in the box and the machine into the boot of the car he said, 'I think every person is a missionary'.

Every Christian is called to Mission on the basis of the Sacrament of Baptism – that God calls people in order to let them participate in his plan of salvation for all. That baptismal commitment is constantly renewed in Eucharist. The privilege of being a Christian consists in being called to participate in a special way in the mission of Christ in serving all human beings; this special way assumes that the person called will have a desire within her or him to be part of God's plan of salvation for all creation. The person must have an experience of the intimacy of God as they go out to be 'fishers of men'. This is not a ticket to earning heaven, as most people not baptised will obtain that anyway, but to be part of the Mission of the Son of God. It does mean then that the missioned must have a sense of fire of Christ that He knew on earth. It does mean that people can be impressed by the life of the Christian – particularly in their attitude to others – 'by this shall all know that you are my disciples'.

The Second Vatican Council said that the whole Church is missionary – meaning that Christian vocation must embrace all of creation – and must be truly universal – that all creation must be treasured from the smallest plant, the shortest river to the most challenged section, tribes or communities of human beings.

The challenge is how do I look on all these beings – hopefully not with my own love but with the love of God for me. The newness of Jesus' Mission was that He saw and experienced the unconditional love of the Father.

How do we participate in making the 'New Heaven' and the 'New Earth'. In short I am called to start thinking and acting as Jesus did:

> To try and make the world a better place,
> To reach out to people in hurt and prejudice and driven to fundamentalism,
> To understand their hurt and be ready to allow Christ's healing to enter,
> and eventually to dialogue with them,

# MISSION

> Not to be afraid of difference – but to cherish it, to realise that all the different peoples coming into these islands now are a rich addition and should be integrated into our growing self-confident community.

Every foreign missionary I've met – and most emigrants – tells me that they learned more about their own culture when they left home than they ever knew when they were at home. People at home now have the opportunity of seeing other people at close hand living their lives, celebrating their great events and worshipping their way. Not alone does it give the host people an opportunity to appreciate others, but it also helps them to cherish and understand their own systems.

Mission is also to see the world as God of Exodus (3:7-9) does – where He takes sides, the side of the poor – and to possess the attitude of being with them in their journey to freedom. A good sign of being in solidarity with the brokenness of people is if we are prepared to work with them rather than work for them – to apply the politics of creativity rather than the politics of salvation. In short, to help people create their own salvation by helping them to help themselves.

God has chosen people to do things for Him by doing things with people and appreciating them and their environment. We need to have the 'mind of Christ' and be like St Columbanus – the great Irish Missionary – whose mantra was 'that we belong to Christ not to ourselves'.

Our taking part in Eucharist is our best affirmation of this. Truly, every Christian can be a missionary.